SOUP
BROTH
BREAD

Rachel Allen

Photography by *Maja Smend* and *Joanne Murphy*
Illustrations by *Jessica Hart*

MICHAEL JOSEPH

MICHAEL JOSEPH

UK | USA | Canada | Ireland | Australia
India | New Zealand | South Africa

Michael Joseph is part of the Penguin Random House group of companies
whose addresses can be found at global.penguinrandomhouse.com

First published by Michael Joseph, 2021

004

Copyright © Rachel Allen, 2021
Photography
© Maja Smend, 2021 (all images not listed below)
© Joanne Murphy, 2021 (pages 4, 8, 17, 22, 23, 30, 35, 38, 41, 49, 70, 71, 77, 78,
89, 93, 111, 113, 118, 129, 132, 161, 167, 181, 197, 201, 231, 267, 269, 271, 276)
Illustrations © Jessica Hart, 2021

Set in Freight Text Pro, Agenda Bold and Recoleta
Colour reproduction by Altaimage Ltd
Printed and bound in Malaysia by Times Offset (M) Sdn. Bhd.

The authorized representative in the EEA is Penguin Random House Ireland,
Morrison Chambers, 32 Nassau Street, Dublin D02 YH68

A CIP catalogue record for this book is available from the British Library

isbn: 978-0-241-48629-0

www.greenpenguin.co.uk

MIX
Paper | Supporting
responsible forestry
FSC® C018179

Penguin Random House is committed to a
sustainable future for our business, our readers
and our planet. This book is made from Forest
Stewardship Council® certified paper.

Contents

soup broth bread

Introduction

Anyone who knows me knows that I am passionate about soup! There's no better food to warm the heart and restore the soul. Whether it's smooth and silky, rustic and chunky or light and brothy, soup conjures up feelings of cosiness and care for me. When I was a child, my mum always had a pot of chicken or turkey stock on the go, ready to work its magic in one of her great soups for when my sister, Simone, and I got in from school. It not only fed our bellies, it fed our hearts, and turned us into avid soup-makers, too.

Now, my own home is filled with soup appreciators. It's the first thing I offer to our children if they're feeling under the weather (after a hug, of course!). Soup helps soothe everything from a sniffly cold to a tired body after a tough day. Our daughter even takes broth or soup in a flask for her school lunch, a little bit of home from home.

Nearly every country and culture has soup at its heart. And few foods have travelled so globally – you're nearly guaranteed to find ramen, chowder, laksa, pho and minestrone in any city. You can traverse the world just through soup. It comes steeped in tradition, too. In Morocco, many Muslims eat fragrant, nourishing harira to break Ramadan. Chicken soup is taken very seriously in millions of Jewish homes across the world and is administered for everything from mild heartache to full-on flu (hence its nickname, 'Jewish penicillin'). Even lovers' tiffs and family feuds have been calmed over gazpacho in Spain and borscht in Russia. Soup is the ultimate fixer.

There's an age-old South American proverb that says, 'Good broth will resurrect the dead.' And indeed, years ago when a dear relative of mine was really unwell, homemade organic chicken broth seemed to have magical effects that had our whole family delightfully flummoxed. Whether it was the placebo effect from being cared for or the fact that it was easily digestible that enabled it to work its spell, we'll never know.

Soup is so steeped into the fabric of my family's life that I roast a chicken at least once a week, in part for the ritual of making fresh stock. I believe that if you're going to invest in good meat and vegetables, then it makes sense to get the maximum value out of it all. There is no better way to extract all the goodness from the leftover bones than to boil them up with nourishing vegetables and aromatic herbs. The nutrients can really help to boost our immune system, our gut, our brains, hormones, skin, and of course our mood.

Making stocks, soups and broths is almost a state of mind. I love having a rummage in the fridge and seeing what needs to be used up and turned into a soup. It's spontaneous and creative and a terrific way of learning how different flavours work together, as well as being a great way to make the most of leftovers. There are tips in this book on using leftovers, as so many cooked vegetables can be turned into a soup once you have just a few other ingredients to hand. Cooked meat and seafood can also be transformed into a chunky broth or chowder with a little know-how, and leftover rice and pasta just love being given another lease of life in a beautiful bowl of soup.

Alongside my recipes for soups, which are sorted by the season, you'll also find recipes for beautiful accompaniments and garnishes to bling up your bowl. Different sauces, salsas, drizzles, oils and emulsions will liven up even the simplest soup, not to mention delicious crackers, croutons and crumbs. You'll discover loads of them here, and suggestions for which soup to serve them with. And of course there is also a whole chapter of wonderful breads, plus savoury buns, flatbreads, scones and muffins, including recipes for particular dietary needs. All perfect to serve with a steaming bowl of soup, or simply to eat warm from the oven.

You'll also find inspiration for presenting your photo-worthy soup, as well as tips for storing and freezing (not all are happy on ice!) and some of my other golden rules, plus a useful list of handy equipment for preparing your soups, broths, breads and garnishes with ease.

Please join me on this soup adventure. I hope this book brings you, your family and your friends much joy for many years to come.

Rachel Allen

Essential soup equipment

You don't need much equipment to make a delicious bowl of soup, but there are various bits of kitchen kit that will certainly make life a whole lot easier if you do have them.

For any cooked soup of course you need a *saucepan*, and a selection of sizes is preferable, depending on what you're making and for how many. With saucepans of all sizes, you tend to get what you pay for, so if you can, try to invest in pots that have good, heavy bases. They'll be easier to cook with, you'll be less likely to burn your food (to a certain degree!) and they'll last a lifetime – or more – if they're of decent quality. If you ever happen to be offered any copper saucepans, accept immediately! They not only look beautiful but are wonderfully heavy in the base and make cooking a dream.

A *large pot* is handy for making up batches of stock, but you can get by using a medium pot that holds just about 4 litres. A good strong *sieve or colander* is invaluable for straining your stocks.

A couple of pint or litre *liquid measures* are really handy in the kitchen, as is a good selection of *mixing bowls*. And anyone who cooks knows that a few *good-quality knives* are essential. It's also really worth buying a *knife steel* to keep your blades sharp.

I adore *wooden chopping boards* and seem to collect them in different shapes and sizes. My main chopping board is one that we were given as a wedding present over 20 years ago and it's still perfect! Go for a large, thick chopping board and scrub it regularly with salt (every couple of weeks) to give it a really thorough clean. Dry it standing upright after washing to prevent it warping.

soup broth bread

Some notes on ingredients

With the basic ingredients that you may always have in your kitchen, you'll never go hungry, as a delicious and nutritious bowl of soup can be made from just a potato, an onion, some butter or olive oil and a bit of stock. Add to that some cream or milk, fresh herbs and a great bit of bread and you have a meal fit for a king or queen.

I always use fresh herbs over dried for goodness and flavour, and don't forget that making pestos and your own flavoured oils will preserve fresh herbs beautifully.

I prefer to buy my dried spices whole (with the exception of dried turmeric, ginger, cayenne and paprika) and grind them as I need them, as this way the flavour is incomparable.

When it comes to fats, I use butter a lot in the kitchen for its delicious goodness, but I also use extra virgin olive oil for many recipes with a Mediterranean flavour. Coconut oil (virgin if possible) is great to use in the kitchen in some Asian recipes, and it has a high smoke point too, which is handy. I'm not overly keen on cooking with vegetable oil, so I tend to use a light extra virgin olive oil, coconut oil or butter in its place.

There are always two types of salt in my kitchen: a fine sea salt and also sea salt flakes. I use the fine salt for seasoning but I love to use the flakes of salt at the table, and also for scattering over the top of breads and some soups if I want a little crunch.

Because I make chicken stock invariably every week, I always have some in the fridge or freezer, but for emergencies I normally have some stock cubes to hand as well. I like to use organic stock cubes. I recommend chicken stock for so many of the recipes. Chicken stock is so versatile with many different flavours, but do keep in mind that if you have another type of stock and want to use it, it'll probably work perfectly provided it's not too strong in flavour. Fish stock is the only stock that I don't use in place of chicken or vegetable stocks, as the flavour is too pronounced, unless it's for a fish soup.

If you have saved bones and vegetables for stock but don't have the time or inclination to make the stock today, don't throw them away. Pop them into the freezer for another day, and you can add more bones and vegetables, be they frozen or not, raw or cooked, to the lot that you have frozen.

You might find it handy to keep in the freezer some ingredients that you use less often. I have a tub of curry leaves in the freezer that I use for some South Indian soups, but not on a regular basis. Pine nuts are handy to store in the freezer too, as they can go rancid quite quickly. And if you have a glut of chillies in your fridge that you're not going to get through, pop them into the freezer for a day when you need a spicy kick in your soup.

Finally, a note on using leftovers. Soups and broths can be a brilliant way to use up what might otherwise be thrown out, particularly surplus cooked vegetables. I'll sometimes use up leftover mashed potato in a soup (it's ideal in the potato, parsley and thyme soup on page 123) – just add it later in the cooking than you would if using raw potato. Soups like this can easily be turned into a new recipe with an assortment of other vegetables thrown in too. Cooked carrots, broccoli, parsnips or even spinach can be added towards the end, keeping in mind that depending on the type of soup you may need an extra bit of liquid to balance out the additional ingredients.

Leftover cooked rice, pasta and even noodles can be given another lease of life by adding them to soup, for example putting small pasta or even rice into a soup such as the Greek lemon chicken soup (see page 48), or cut-up spaghetti in the pork and fennel meatball soup (see page 114). Just make sure to mix it in towards the end of the cooking time, giving it just enough time to reheat but not to overcook. And don't forget leftover cooked meat and seafood. Adding it to a soup is a simple but delicious way to stop it going to waste.

Key
Recipes marked with a 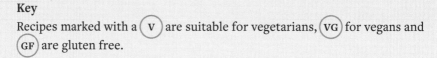 ⓥ are suitable for vegetarians, ⓥɢ for vegans and ɢꜰ are gluten free.

Storing and freezing soup

Whether it's for a quick lunch on the run, or a cosy supper, I'm always so grateful if I have soup in the fridge. Most soups will keep well refrigerated for a few days, as long as the ingredients used are fresh to begin with. Keep them covered to avoid other aromas tainting the soup.

I love having soup in the freezer and will often purposely make more than I need so that I can put some away for a rainy day. Most soups will freeze, with the exception of those that contain a liaison, like the garlic soup on page 180 (though if made up to the stage just before adding the liaison, it will freeze perfectly – add the liaison later, once the soup is defrosted), or those that contain eggs, such as the egg drop soup on page 54 (though, again, this will freeze well if brought just to the point before adding the egg). Noodle soups like the Japanese noodle broth on page 31 or the laksa on page 178 also don't do well in the freezer, so bring them just to the point of adding the noodles before freezing, then cook the noodles fresh when serving and don't add the final garnishes until the last moment.

Smooth blended soups freeze very well, and chunky broths will still be good after freezing if you're careful when reheating not to break up the bits and pieces. All stocks freeze perfectly, and if you're short of freezer space it's a good idea to make your own stock cubes. Do this by placing the strained and degreased stock in a saucepan and boiling it, uncovered, until it reduces down to a strong-tasting liquid, about one-tenth of its original volume, or even less. Pour into ice cube trays and freeze. When you need stock, just take out one or two cubes and mix with some boiling water, as you would a powdered stock cube.

Many of the breads in this book can be frozen, but just remember, a bread will only be (almost) as good as it was when it went into the freezer, so freeze it when it's as fresh as possible. Leftover stale bread is of course what you need for breadcrumbs, so rather than throwing out the end of a loaf you can cut off the crusts (or leave them on if you prefer) and whiz up the bread in a food processor or blender, then use straight away or pop into the freezer for another day.

As mentioned, keep by and save any tubs and lids that can be used for storing and freezing soup. Depending on how many people you're regularly feeding, you might find it handier to freeze soup in a few small containers rather than one large one. A good indelible pen and stickers or masking tape are invaluable for labelling, of course, as although we always think we'll remember what's in the tubs in the freezer, three months on it's almost impossible! Remember to write the date as well as the type of soup so you'll know how long it's been in there for.

Presenting your soups

There are so many more ways to serve soup other than just a big deep bowl (though certainly I'll never complain about a big bowl of soup!).

You can make an edible bread bowl out of a small, round, hollowed-out loaf of crusty white yeast bread if you wish, though do keep in mind that this works best for a slightly thicker soup, like the potato, parsley and thyme soup (see page 123) or the pork and fennel meatball soup (see page 114), rather than for a broth which can leak out quickly. Just slice off the top of the loaf, reserving this to use as a lid, then scoop out the insides of the bread (you can whiz this in a food processor or liquidizer to make breadcrumbs for another recipe – these can be frozen) and fill with the soup, topping it with the lid to serve. Enjoy the soup, then eat the bread afterwards – it will be deliciously soggy and flavoursome on the inside!

Hollowed-out butternut squash work really well as soup bowls too. If you're making a soup with the flesh, such as the curried butternut squash soup (see page 120), just slice the top off the butternut squash horizontally, then use a spoon and a sharp knife to scoop out the flesh and seeds from inside the skin. Use the flesh (without the seeds) for the soup, then roast the hollowed-out butternut squash shell and its lid in a hot oven for 5–10 minutes, depending on the size of the butternut squash. You want to just cook the skin but it should not be so well cooked that the shell collapses. Pour the soup inside and serve to your delighted guests. This can work with one large butternut squash as a bowl to serve up from in the middle of the table, or with small squashes used as individual bowls.

There are many other fruits and vegetables that can be transformed into a soup bowl – your imagination is the only limitation! Think hollowed-out watermelon (for the watermelon gazpacho on page 97 or for holding the watermelon, mint and gin soup shots on page 94, a bit like a punch bowl), think peppers for the roasted red pepper and basil soup on page 61 (as recommended for the butternut squash bowl, I would partially roast these after scooping out the seeds), and even large, scooped-out tomatoes to hold lovely chilled servings of salmorejo (see page 58).

Having a party? Shot glasses and espresso cups are great for serving soup canapés, no matter what the soup. They're easy to serve, and hot soup canapés are a great little warmer in wintertime.

You may have all kinds of things at home that could potentially make your soup presentation a little more interesting and attractive. If you're lucky enough to have a selection of small copper saucepans they look beautiful for serving soup, as do cute glass jars such as Kilner jars. I love collecting vintage glasses and adore how pretty a selection of lots of different ones can look on a table with something like tomato and basil water (see page 92) inside.

I'm a big fan of a flask and have a nice little selection of them at home for enjoying soups and stews or coffee from while on the go – and even a little hot whiskey from time to time! A tall, narrow flask is great for keeping soup warm for hours, ready to pour into a bowl when you're at work or school, whereas a wide food flask is ideal if you're having a picnic or are on the run, so to speak, and need to eat directly from it with a spoon.

When it comes to serving up your homemade bread, if you're going to slice it at the table then of course a board is the best option, but I also love baskets, trays and even large flat stones foraged from the beach. If I am ever at the beach and spy some lovely shells, I always hang on to them and wash them well, then I use them for serving butter, salt, pestos and other accompaniments.

A bowl of soup can be as simple as that, and so lovely and comforting for it, but with extra accompaniments and garnishes you can really get creative with your serving and presentation ideas and there's a whole world of inspiration to explore, so turn to page 187 for some more ideas.

SPRING

Simple chicken meatball soup with orzo

Serves 4–6

A simple and uncomplicated soup, this relies on good chicken stock and delicious, flavoursome meatballs. Orzo, also known as risoni, is a small shaped pasta, not much bigger than a grain of rice. Indeed, rice could replace the pasta for a gluten-free version of this clean restorative soup.

150g orzo

400g skinless chicken breast (see note)

3 large cloves of garlic, crushed or finely grated

1 generous tablespoon chopped sage

salt and freshly ground pepper

2 tablespoons extra virgin olive oil, plus a drizzle for the top

1 litre chicken stock (see page 264)

2 tablespoons chopped parsley

Place a saucepan of water on a high heat with a few good pinches of salt. When it comes to the boil, add the orzo and stir as the water comes back to the boil. Cook the orzo for 8 minutes, or until tender, then drain, rinse with cold water and set aside.

While the orzo is cooking, cut the chicken breast meat into chunks, free of any skin or membrane. Place it in a food processor and blend until the meat is finely minced. Tip the meat into a bowl, add the garlic and the chopped sage, and season with salt and pepper. Place a frying pan on a medium heat and drizzle in a little olive oil. Take a small piece, about half a teaspoon, of the chicken mixture and fry it for a couple of minutes, turning it halfway through. Taste and add more seasoning if necessary.

Now shape the remaining mixture into meatballs, each about 15g in weight – you should get about 26 balls altogether. Fry them in the olive oil over a medium heat, turning them regularly, until they're cooked on the inside (they'll have a firm spring) and golden all over.

Bring the chicken stock to the boil in a saucepan and add the cooked orzo, the meatballs and the chopped parsley. Season to taste.

Serve in warm bowls, with a small drizzle of extra virgin olive oil over the top.

note   *If you prefer, you can just buy minced chicken from your butcher.*

Spring – **soup** broth bread

Wild garlic broth

Serves 4–6

The rich allium aroma of wild garlic in shaded woodlands is one that I adore. A true sign of spring and of all the delicious and super-nutritious foods just waiting to be foraged and turned into wonderful treats.

This soup is just what I long for when the wild garlic is out. It's so special, as you can only pick or buy it when it's in season. For the true wild garlic flavour, seek out Allium ursinum, also known as ramsons, wood garlic or buckrams. Another variety is the long-, thin-leaved Allium triquetrum, also known as three-cornered leek, which is less garlicky and slightly more leeky in flavour but also delicious.

Just remember – as with all wild foraged foods, if they're not in your garden, don't pick the root, just snip or pick what's above the ground to allow for regrowth.

(VG) (GF)

2 tablespoons extra virgin olive oil

175g peeled and finely diced potatoes

150g peeled and finely diced onions

salt and freshly ground pepper

250g wild garlic leaves

1 litre vegetable or chicken stock (see pages 277, 264)

Pour the olive oil into a saucepan and place over a medium heat. Add the diced potatoes and onions, season with salt and pepper and stir to mix. Reduce the heat to low, cover with a piece of parchment paper and the saucepan lid, and cook for 7 minutes, stirring gently every so often to prevent the potatoes sticking.

While the vegetables are cooking, wash the wild garlic leaves in cold water, then drain and toss dry, either in a colander, a clean tea towel or a salad spinner. Chop the leaves quite finely and set aside.

Once the vegetables have been cooking for 7 minutes, add the stock, bring to the boil over a high heat, then add the chopped wild garlic leaves and cook, uncovered, for just 1–2 minutes, until the leaves are tender. Taste for seasoning and serve, or set aside then reheat when you're ready to serve.

note *A few drops of a fruity extra virgin olive oil are delicious drizzled over the broth when serving, if you wish.*

Mediterranean fish soup with rouille

Serves 4–6

This is a wonderfully luxurious and decadent soup. It takes a while, and lots of fish, to make, but it is worth every single minute. If you don't have every type of seafood, that's no problem, just use more of the others, but if you can get a variety of fish and shellfish it does bring such delicious flavours. Just make sure to only use what is really good and fresh and as whole as possible, as the bones and heads contain so much goodness and flavour.

The rouille is a divinely rich emulsion sauce, much like a mayonnaise, but made with bread, cayenne and saffron. It can be made earlier in the day, or even 24 hours in advance if necessary.

2.5kg whole fish, flat or round (remove the gills or ask your fishmonger to do it, but leave the heads on if possible)

1 large crab

12 mussels (see notes)

12 whole prawns, heads included if possible

100ml extra virgin olive oil

300g chopped onion

2 cloves of garlic, finely grated or crushed

salt and freshly ground pepper

5 large ripe tomatoes, or 1 x 400g tin of plum tomatoes, chopped

1 teaspoon sugar

3 sprigs of fennel

stalks from 3 sprigs of parsley (keep the leaves for garnish)

2 sprigs of thyme

1 bay leaf

750ml fish stock (see page 272)

a pinch of cayenne pepper

a pinch of saffron

juice of ¼ to ½ a lemon

For the rouille

25g white bread, such as baguette, crusts removed

4 tablespoons hot fish stock (see page 272)

3 cloves of garlic, crushed or finely grated

1 large egg yolk

a pinch of cayenne pepper

a pinch of saffron

salt and freshly ground pepper

75g extra virgin olive oil

For the croutons

6–8 slices of baguette, cut at an angle, 6–8mm thick (it can be slightly stale)

100g grated Gruyère cheese

To serve

1 tablespoon chopped parsley

Cut the whole fish into chunks, with the heads still on if possible (you need to be not squeamish for this – it'll be worth it). Set aside with the crab, mussels and prawns.

Heat the olive oil in a large saucepan over a high heat. Add the onions and garlic, season with salt and pepper, then turn the heat down to low and cover the pan with a lid. Cook for 8–10 minutes, until the onions are tender. Now add the chopped tomatoes (leaving the skins on if they're fresh ones), sugar, fennel, parsley stalks, thyme and bay leaf, then the fish chunks and raw crab, mussels and prawns, including all the shells. Season with salt and pepper, turn the heat up to high and cook, covered, for 10 minutes. Add the fish stock, bring back to the boil and cook for a further 10 minutes.

Take the pan off the heat and carefully pick out the mussel shells and the crab shells, as these will be too hard to be mashed. Take the mussels from the shells, discarding the shells, and put the mussels into the soup. Remove the crab meat from the body and the claws, and add to the soup also. Add the cayenne and the saffron.

Now push the soup through a mouli-legumes (see notes) into a bowl underneath (this can take a few minutes of hard work but eventually you'll be left with a mass of dry bones in the strainer part, which you discard). Place the strained soup in a saucepan, reheat it, and add a little more fish stock if it is too thick. Taste for seasoning, adding a squeeze of lemon juice if it needs it.

To make the rouille, cut the bread into cubes and soak in the hot fish stock in a bowl for 5 minutes. It should be soggy but not wet, so squeeze out any excess liquid if there is any, then, using a fork, mash the bread in the bowl. Add the crushed or finely grated garlic, the egg yolk, a pinch of cayenne and the saffron. Season with salt and pepper. Mix well and pour in the olive oil *very* slowly, in a very thin, steady stream, while whisking constantly, as if making a mayonnaise.

To make the croutons, simply toast the slices of baguette on both sides.

To serve, reheat the soup, and while it is reheating, spread the croutons with rouille and sprinkle with the grated Gruyère cheese. Pour the hot soup into warm bowls and float a crouton on top of each. Scatter over the chopped parsley and serve.

notes   *Scrub the mussels clean under cold running water, discarding any that are open and do not close when tapped on the work surface.*

If you have a powerful blender you can blend the soup, once the mussel and crab shells have been removed, then just strain it through a sieve.

Beetroot and tahini soup

Serves 6

The vivid colour of this soup alone will certainly put a pep in your step. I love the sweet, earthy beetroot and nutty tahini combination. It's so simple, yet very pleasing. Make a big batch of the soup if you have lots of beetroot and freeze it for a day when you need cheering up.

2 tablespoons extra virgin olive oil

1 large onion, chopped

2 cloves of garlic, chopped

salt and freshly ground pepper

450g beetroot (5 medium beetroot)

800ml vegetable or chicken stock
  (see pages 277, 264)

75g tahini

For the tahini sauce

50g tahini

1 large clove of garlic, crushed or
  finely grated

2 teaspoons toasted and ground
  cumin seeds

2 tablespoons extra virgin olive oil

1 tablespoon lemon juice

50–75ml water

For the garnish

1 teaspoon toasted and ground
  cumin seeds

coriander leaves

Pour the olive oil into a saucepan over a medium heat and add the chopped onion and garlic. Season with salt and pepper, then reduce the heat to low, cover the pan with a lid and cook the onions very gently for 8–10 minutes, until tender, stirring from time to time.

Peel the beetroot and cut into approximately 1cm dice, then add to the onions with the stock and season with salt and pepper. Bring to the boil, then lower the heat a bit and cook for 30 minutes or until the beetroot is tender. Add the tahini, then blend the soup until smooth. Check the seasoning and add more salt and pepper if necessary.

To make the tahini sauce, place the tahini in a bowl and add the garlic, cumin, olive oil and lemon juice. Whisk well to blend, adding just enough water to give a thick cream-like drizzling consistency. Season to taste and set aside.

Serve the soup steaming hot, with the tahini sauce drizzled over the top. Sprinkle with toasted ground cumin and add a scattering of coriander leaves.

Spring – soup **broth** bread

Japanese chicken and udon noodle broth

Serves 4

I adore this clean, fresh and super-quick broth, and the flavours bring back fond memories of a wonderful trip I took around Japan. Udon noodles are thick, wheat-flour noodles often served in a broth, though you can also use the thinner soba noodles, or for a gluten-free version rice noodles will also work.

This soup calls for dashi, a Japanese stock which you can make easily yourself (see page 274), or buy ready-made. However, you can replace the dashi with chicken stock, and while it will be different, it will still be lovely.

2 small, or 1 medium, skinless chicken breasts, thinly sliced

5 tablespoons mirin (Japanese rice wine)

2cm piece of fresh ginger, bashed with a rolling pin but still in one piece

75g udon noodles

1 litre dashi or chicken stock (see pages 274, 264)

4 tablespoons Japanese soy sauce, such as Kikkoman

150g mangetout, topped and tailed, or 2 small courgettes (12cm long), halved lengthwise then cut into thin slices at an angle

2 spring onions, sliced thinly at an angle

Place the chicken in a bowl with 2 tablespoons of mirin and the bashed piece of ginger and toss lightly to coat.

Bring a large saucepan of water to the boil, drop in the noodles and stir to prevent them from sticking. Bring back to the boil and cook for 6–9 minutes (this will depend on the brand of noodles that you're using) until almost tender (udon noodles should retain a little bit of bite, like 'al dente' pasta). Lower a cup into the water to reserve about half a cupful of the liquid, then drain the noodles in a sieve. If you want to keep the noodles standing for any longer than 3 minutes you should put them back in the empty saucepan, adding a few tablespoons of the cooking liquid to stop them sticking. Just add more liquid, another tablespoon or two, if the noodles start sticking at any stage.

Pour the dashi (or chicken stock) into a saucepan, add the remaining 3 tablespoons of mirin and the soy sauce and bring to the boil. Add the chicken and cook for just

▶

2 minutes. Skim any impurities from the surface. Add the mangetout or courgette slices and continue to cook for 1 more minute, or until the chicken and vegetables are cooked. Strain the chicken and vegetables, pouring the broth into a sieve lined with kitchen paper and letting it filter through slowly – this will ensure a clear and glossy broth. To speed up this process, I normally use two sieves, each lined with kitchen paper and sitting over a bowl.

When you're ready to serve, divide the noodles among your serving bowls. Reheat the broth, taste for seasoning and add another tablespoon of soy sauce if needed. Ladle the broth with some chicken and vegetables over the udon noodles in the bowls and sprinkle with sliced spring onions.

Mexican chicken broth with avocado and coriander salsa

Serves 4–6

I love this clean and uplifting soup, which is full of marvellous Mexican flavours. The success of this recipe rests on having a good chicken stock at its base. To prepare it in advance, make the soup up to (but not including) the stage of adding the chicken, store in the fridge for a day or two, then cook the chicken and make the salsa just before serving.

3 tablespoons extra virgin olive oil

1 onion, peeled and finely chopped

salt and freshly ground pepper

3 large cloves of garlic, peeled and finely chopped

1 teaspoon deseeded and finely chopped red chilli

1 litre chicken stock (see page 264)

1 large skinless chicken breast, diced into 1cm pieces

juice of ½ a lime

For the salsa

3 spring onions, finely sliced

1 ripe avocado, peeled, stoned and diced into 5mm pieces

150g tomatoes (or cherry tomatoes), diced into 5mm pieces

juice of ½ a lime

2 tablespoons chopped coriander leaves

Heat the olive oil in a saucepan over a medium heat, add the chopped onion and season with salt and pepper. Cover with a butter wrapper or a piece of parchment paper and the saucepan lid, then turn the heat down to low and cook for 10 minutes, stirring once or twice, until the onion is soft.

Add the garlic and chilli and cook for 2 minutes. Now add the stock and bring to the boil, reduce to a simmer, then add in the chicken and gently cook for 3–4 minutes, until the meat is cooked. Turn off the heat, then add the lime juice and season to taste.

Make the salsa by mixing all the ingredients together, then season with salt and pepper.

To serve, ladle the hot soup into warm bowls and drop a large tablespoon of the salsa into each bowl.

Sea beet broth
with green pesto

Sea beet, also sometimes called wild spinach or sea spinach, is a wonderful green leafy vegetable that can be found all year round on beaches in Ireland and around the British coast. It's an ancestor of beetroot, chard and sugar beet, and has been revered for many years for its high nutritional properties. The flavour is not unlike chard or spinach, but with, unsurprisingly, a slightly salty, beachy tang.

I love to use the young new leaves in spring for soups, broths and sauces. This recipe is for a restorative broth served with a liberal drizzle of green pesto over the top, or you can alternatively make a smooth blended soup out of this fabulous foraged vegetable, like the spinach and rosemary soup on page 46.

2 tablespoons extra virgin olive oil

150g peeled and finely diced onions

150g peeled and finely diced potatoes

salt and freshly ground pepper

750ml vegetable or chicken stock (see pages 277, 264)

250g sea beet (stalks removed before weighing), chopped finely

To serve

parsley pesto or kale and hazelnut pesto (see page 198)

Place the olive oil in a saucepan over a medium heat. Add the diced onions and potatoes, season with salt and pepper, stir, then cover with a butter wrapper or a piece of parchment paper and the saucepan lid. Turn the heat down to low and cook gently for 10 minutes, stirring every now and again.

After 10 minutes, pour the stock into the pan, turn the heat up to high and bring to the boil. Check that the potatoes and onions are tender – if not, cook them for a couple of minutes longer until they are.

Now tip in the chopped sea beet, season with salt and pepper, and cook, uncovered, over a high heat for 1–2 minutes, or until the sea beet is tender. As soon as it is cooked, take the pan off the heat and don't cover it again while the soup is hot or you may lose the rich verdant colour.

Taste for seasoning, and serve in warm bowls with a drizzle of pesto over the top.

notes

This soup freezes well.

To prevent the soup losing its fresh colour and flavour, it's important to reheat it without the lid on, and also to avoid prolonged simmering.

Carrot and harissa soup with za'atar croutons

Serves 4–6

Sweet carrots love the spicy kick of harissa, the Tunisian chilli paste, in this delicious and colourful soup that's enhanced by za'atar croutons. Halloumi cheese makes a great gluten-free alternative to the croutons, if you prefer. Just toss chunks with olive oil and za'atar, and roast for 5–6 minutes, until golden. Like so many others, this soup freezes really well (without the croutons).

2 tablespoons extra virgin olive oil

175g peeled and chopped onions

1 large clove of garlic, finely chopped

350g peeled and diced carrots

salt and freshly ground pepper

3 teaspoons harissa paste (see page 194)

750ml vegetable or chicken stock (see pages 277, 264)

juice of ½ a lemon

For the za'atar croutons

3 thick slices of white yeast bread (Japanese shokupan (page 248) or challah would also work well)

2 tablespoons extra virgin olive oil

2 generous teaspoons za'atar

To serve

2 teaspoons thick natural yoghurt

a few coriander leaves

Pour the olive oil into a saucepan over a medium to high heat and add the chopped onions, garlic and carrots. Season with salt and freshly ground pepper and toss until coated. Cover with a butter paper or a piece of parchment paper and a saucepan lid. Turn the heat down to low and cook gently for about 10 minutes, stirring regularly, until the vegetables have almost softened.

Remove the lid and paper, stir in the harissa and turn the heat up. Pour in the stock and boil until the veg is completely tender. Pour into a liquidizer and blend until smooth. Add lemon juice and more salt and pepper to taste – it may even need more harissa.

To make the croutons, cut the crusts off the bread and cut the bread into 1.5cm cubes. Toss in a bowl with the olive oil and za'atar, seasoning with salt and pepper. Spread the croutons out on a baking tray, in a single layer, and cook in an oven preheated to 220°C/200°C fan/gas 7 for 5–6 minutes, until golden and crisp.

Serve the steaming hot soup in warm bowls, with little blobs of yoghurt, a scattering of coriander leaves, and a few croutons on each.

notes *If you don't want to turn on the oven just for the croutons, you can sauté them in a frying pan, tossing regularly, instead.*

If you have some leftover cooked carrots, they can be used in place of some or all of the carrots in the recipe here. Add with the stock and continue as above.

Lovage, pea, cucumber and bacon soup

Serves 4–6

In this summery soup, the sweet peas and refreshing cucumber are enhanced by the herb lovage. Easy to grow yourself, yet tricky to find in a supermarket, the flavour of lovage is very savoury, much like that of its close relative, celery. Use mint, tarragon or coriander in its place if you can't get hold of it. I love the addition of bacon to this soup, but feel free to leave it out if you prefer.

100g streaky bacon rashers, cut into lardons
150g finely chopped onions
salt and freshly ground pepper
850ml chicken stock (see page 264)

200g peas (I use good frozen peas)
½ a cucumber, finely diced
1 tablespoon roughly chopped lovage, plus a few extra whole lovage leaves for garnish
75ml cream (regular or double)

Place a saucepan on a medium to low heat and immediately add the bacon lardons. Allow them to cook slowly for about 3 minutes, so that the fat renders out and the bacon becomes golden and crispy.

Spoon the bacon out of the pan, setting it aside for later, but leaving all the bacon fat in the pan. Add the chopped onions, season with salt and pepper, cover with a butter wrapper or a piece of parchment paper, then put on the lid and cook over a low heat for 8–10 minutes, until the onions are tender, stirring every so often. If there's not very much fat from the bacon in the pan, you can add 1 tablespoon of olive oil to stop the onions sticking.

Now add the stock, turn up the heat to high and bring to the boil. Add the peas and finely diced cucumber and cook very rapidly, making sure to remove the lid as soon as it comes to the boil, for only 3 or 4 minutes, or until the peas and cucumber are cooked.

As soon as the peas are cooked, use a sieve to remove about 2 tablespoons of the peas and cucumber and set aside, leaving all the liquid in the pan. Add the chopped lovage to the pan and immediately blend the soup with the cream until smooth.

Check the seasoning and adjust if necessary.

Pour the steaming hot soup into bowls, then spoon the bacon lardons and the peas and cucumber dice over the top. Scatter over a few snipped lovage leaves, and serve.

Asparagus and tarragon soup

Serves 4–6

This is a perfect soup for spring, when both asparagus and tarragon are in season. Light and smooth, yet wonderfully flavoursome, this gorgeous green soup uses anise-like tarragon to complement the rich nuttiness of asparagus spears. Use chervil or mint in place of tarragon if you wish. As with all green soups, avoid prolonged boiling and reheating to retain colour and flavour.

50g butter
125g chopped onions
salt and freshly ground pepper
500g asparagus
850ml hot chicken stock
  (see page 264)

2 teaspoons chopped tarragon
150ml cream (regular or double)

To serve
2 tablespoons very softly
  whipped cream

Melt the butter in a saucepan over a medium heat and when it foams add the chopped onions. Season with salt and pepper, stir to mix, then cover with a butter wrapper or a piece of parchment paper and the saucepan lid. Turn the heat down to low and cook over a gentle heat for 10 minutes, until the onions are completely tender and translucent.

While the onions are cooking, snap off and discard the tough woody end from the base of each asparagus spear – it should snap just a few centimetres up from the base – using your fingers. Now cut off the decorative tips (the top 3 or 4cm) from the asparagus and set aside for later.

Cut the remaining asparagus into thin slices, about 5mm thick, and add to the onions. Stir over the heat and cook for 2 minutes, then turn the heat up to high, add the hot stock, and boil uncovered until the asparagus is tender, about 3–4 minutes. Add the chopped tarragon and the cream and blend the soup until smooth, tasting and correcting the seasoning.

To cook the reserved asparagus tips, bring a small saucepan of water to the boil on a high heat. Add a good pinch of salt, then drop in the asparagus tips and boil, without the lid, for approximately 3 minutes, until just tender. To serve, gently reheat the soup, keeping it uncovered, then serve in warm bowls with a drizzle of softly whipped cream over the top and a scattering of the cooked asparagus tips.

Italian wedding soup

I always had the romantic notion that this soup was served at Italian weddings. I had heard that it was served to give the newly wedded couple energy for their nuptial night. Alas, this hearty soup of meatballs, pasta and vegetables cooked in a rich chicken broth has nothing to do with brides, grooms and romance as such, but was originally called *minestra maritata* in Italian, which actually means 'married soup' because of the way that the green vegetables, the *minestra*, marry with the meat.

The original Italian wedding soup was thought to be a peasant dish made using leftover sausages or meatballs, usually pork, with some greens and other vegetables. Use whichever delicious greens you have. In place of the spinach you can use cabbage, kale, chard, broccoli or bitter greens, such as chicory, escarole or endive.

Try to find a small pasta for this like *acini de pepe* (which means 'seeds of pepper' because of its small round shape), ditalini or orzo. Failing that, you could break up spaghetti into tiny pieces.

For the meatballs
225g minced beef
225g minced pork
50g fresh white breadcrumbs
1 small egg, whisked
50g finely grated Parmesan cheese
2 tablespoons chopped parsley
1 teaspoon chopped marjoram or thyme
salt and freshly ground pepper
1–2 tablespoons extra virgin olive oil

For the soup
2 tablespoons extra virgin olive oil

2 onions, cut into 5mm dice
2 carrots, cut into 5mm dice
4 celery stalks, cut into 5mm dice
4 large cloves of garlic, crushed or finely grated
1.25 litres chicken stock (see page 264)
175g small pasta shapes, such as *acini de pepe* or orzo or ditalini
175g de-stalked spinach (weight when stalks have been removed), chopped

To serve
finely grated Parmesan cheese, approximately 50g

▸

First, make the meatballs. Place the minced meat in a bowl and add the breadcrumbs, whisked egg, Parmesan and chopped herbs. Season with salt and pepper and mix well.

Place a frying pan on a medium heat and add a small drizzle of olive oil. Cook a teaspoonful of the mixture and taste it for seasoning, then adjust the rest with more salt, pepper and herbs if necessary. Once you're happy with the flavour, shape the meat mixture into small meatballs, just about 1.5cm or 2cm in size. Place on a baking tray or plate lined with parchment paper and put into the fridge until you're ready to cook them. (They can be placed in the freezer like this, then, once frozen, transferred into a box with a lid until you're ready to use them.)

When you're ready to cook the meatballs (they can be cooked from frozen), place a wide frying pan on a medium to high heat and allow it to warm up. Add a couple of tablespoons of olive oil, then the meatballs. If the frying pan won't hold all the meatballs in a single layer, you'll need to cook them in a couple of batches. Cook the meatballs, turning the heat down to medium once they're sizzling, until they are golden all over and cooked in the centre. Take out of the pan and repeat with the remaining meatballs if you're cooking them in two batches. Set them aside until later.

Now make the soup. Place a large saucepan on a medium heat and add a couple of tablespoons of olive oil. Tip in the chopped onions, carrots and celery, season with salt and pepper, and cover with a lid. Turn the heat down to low and cook slowly, stirring every few minutes, until the vegetables are almost softened.

Add the garlic and cook for 2 minutes more. Add the chicken stock, bring to the boil and season to taste. Now add the pasta and cook over a medium-high heat for 5–8 minutes, depending on the pasta that you are using, until it is almost tender, then add the chopped greens and cook for 2 minutes more.

Finally, tip in the meatballs and allow them to heat up in the broth while the greens are finishing cooking. At this point, the pasta, vegetables and greens should all be cooked and the meatballs should be hot. Ladle into deep warm bowls and grate Parmesan over the top to serve.

 note   *If you are making this in advance you might need to thin it out with a little extra stock, as the pasta tends to absorb the moisture if it sits for a while.*

Spinach and rosemary soup

Serves 6

We've been making this soup at the Ballymaloe Cookery School for many years. I love the rich, verdant flavour of the spinach, which works so well with the rosemary. It's a soup that freezes well, but when reheating, it's important to do so without the lid on, and to avoid prolonged simmering, to prevent the soup losing its intense green colour and flavour. Watercress, chard or kale can all replace the spinach if you wish.

V

GF

15g butter
110g peeled and chopped onions
150g peeled and chopped potatoes
salt and freshly ground pepper
600ml vegetable or chicken stock
    (see pages 277, 264)

275g spinach (stalks removed before weighing), chopped (see notes)
1 tablespoon chopped rosemary
600ml milk, or 500ml milk plus 100ml cream

Melt the butter in a saucepan over a medium heat. Add the chopped onions and potatoes, season with salt and pepper, stir, and cover with a butter wrapper or a piece of parchment paper and the saucepan lid. Turn the heat down to low and cook gently for 10 minutes, stirring every now and again.

After 10 minutes, pour the stock into the saucepan, turn the heat up to high and bring to the boil. Check that the potatoes and onions are tender and, if not, cook them for a couple of minutes longer until they are. Tip in the chopped spinach, season with salt and pepper again, and cook, uncovered, over a high heat for 1–2 minutes, or until the spinach is just cooked. As soon as the spinach is cooked, add the chopped rosemary and take the pan off the heat.

Add the milk, and the cream if using, and blend the soup straight away to preserve the lovely fresh green colour of the spinach. Taste for seasoning, and serve.

notes   *I love to use large-leaved perpetual spinach for this soup; but you can also use baby spinach, in which case there's no need to destalk it.*

To serve this soup broth style, just increase the stock to 750ml, omit the milk and cream, and do not blend.

Greek lemon chicken soup

This is my slightly unorthodox take on a Greek classic, called *avgolemono*, meaning egg-lemon. It's a super-nutritious bowl of goodness where eggs enrich and thicken the broth, giving a silky-smooth soup with orzo pasta, chicken and lots of parsley.

1.6 litres chicken stock (see page 264)

2 celery stalks, cut in half

2 carrots, cut in half

1 leek, trimmed at the base and dark green top discarded

6 black peppercorns

300g skinless chicken breast (2 chicken breasts)

salt and freshly ground pepper

50g orzo

2 eggs

1 teaspoon finely grated lemon zest

2 tablespoons freshly squeezed lemon juice

1 tablespoon finely chopped parsley

25g feta cheese (optional)

Put the chicken stock into a saucepan with the celery and carrots. Cut the leek into big chunks and add them too, then tip in the peppercorns and skinless chicken breasts. Place the pan on a medium to high heat and bring up to a simmer, then turn the heat down to low and allow to simmer for about 15 minutes, until the chicken is just cooked.

Strain into a bowl, discarding the vegetables and peppercorns but reserving the chicken. Pour the strained flavoured broth back into the saucepan and bring back to the boil over a high heat. Season to taste and add the orzo. Boil for about 8–10 minutes, until the orzo is cooked. Meanwhile, slice the chicken very thinly.

While the orzo is still cooking, crack the eggs into a mixing bowl and whisk well. Add the finely grated lemon zest and the lemon juice and mix.

When the orzo is cooked in the broth, take it off the heat and pour about a quarter of the broth on to the egg mixture, whisking all the time. It should look creamy. Pour the egg and broth mixture back into the broth saucepan and add the chicken.

When you're ready to enjoy the soup, place the pan over a low heat and reheat very gently, just until steaming. Be careful not to let the mixture boil at any stage, or the eggs will scramble, leaving you with a lumpy soup.

Ladle into bowls, making sure everyone gets some orzo and chicken, then sprinkle with chopped parsley and crumble over some feta cheese, if using.

 notes   *Sometimes I add two peeled and slightly bashed garlic cloves to this soup if I'm craving a garlicky hit.*

Rice also works well in this soup instead of orzo, for a gluten-free version. It'll take approximately the same amount of time to cook.

Beef and sweet potato goulash soup

Serves 4–6

One of the national dishes of Hungary, goulash is a soup or stew of vegetables and meat that's seasoned with spices. While the spices might vary slightly, a goulash is rarely without paprika, and in this version there's caraway too, which I love for its distinctive nutty, sharp and anise notes.

4 tablespoons extra virgin olive oil

1 large onion, finely sliced

4 cloves of garlic, crushed or finely grated

salt and freshly ground pepper

450g stewing beef, trimmed and cut into fine slices, just 5mm thick

3 teaspoons sweet Hungarian paprika

2 teaspoons toasted and ground caraway seeds

1 sweet potato (approximately 400g in weight) peeled and cut into 1cm dice

1 x 400g tin of plum tomatoes, chopped

1 teaspoon sugar

1 litre beef or chicken stock (see pages 270, 264)

1 red pepper, quartered, deseeded and cut into 1cm dice

2 tablespoons chopped parsley, plus a little more for serving

To serve

3 tablespoons natural yoghurt or crème fraîche

½ teaspoon smoked paprika

Place a large saucepan over a medium heat and add 2 tablespoons of the olive oil. Tip in the sliced onion and the garlic and season with salt and pepper. Turn the heat down to low and cook the onions, uncovered, until tender and lightly golden, about 8–10 minutes. Take the onions out of the saucepan and set aside in a bowl.

Place the saucepan back over a high heat and add another 2 tablespoons of olive oil. When it's hot, tip in the sliced beef, paprika and caraway seeds, and cook, stirring regularly, until the beef has lost its raw red colour. Season, then add in the cooked onions and garlic, as well as the sweet potato dice, tomatoes, sugar and stock.

Bring to the boil, then turn the heat down and simmer, covered with the lid, for 30 minutes. Add the red pepper dice and cook for another 30 minutes, until the beef and vegetables are tender. Season to taste and add three-quarters of the chopped parsley.

Serve the soup with a blob of yoghurt or crème fraîche on the top, a scattering of chopped parsley and finally a pinch of smoked paprika.

Spring – **soup** broth bread

Chinese-style fish soup

We make this soup at the cookery school at Ballymaloe. I love it – it's so light, yet flavoursome and comforting. The base of this soup calls for Chinese stock, which is made from chicken and pork bones, but if you wish you can also use a fish stock, such as the Asian-style fish stock (see page 273).

I find that flat fish works really well, with its delicate flavour and thin fillets that cook very quickly. If you have some extra cooked shellfish such as crab meat, clams, cockles or mussels, they would be divine added in too, along with the shrimps or prawns. Sometimes I like to add a red chilli at the end when serving.

225g flat white fish fillets, such as sole, brill, turbot, John Dory or plaice, skinned

1.5 litres Chinese stock (see page 275)

salt and freshly ground white pepper

18 prawns or 30 small shrimps, cooked and peeled

To serve

1 large handful of shredded iceberg lettuce

2 spring onions, finely sliced at an angle

1 red chilli, deseeded and thinly sliced (optional)

a small handful of coriander leaves

Cut the fish fillets lengthways so that the pieces are 2cm wide, then slice into strips at an angle, 1cm wide.

Bring the stock to the boil, add some salt and pepper (preferably white pepper) to taste, then add the fish slices. Simmer for just 1 minute, then add the prawns or shrimps and allow to heat through.

Divide the shredded lettuce, sliced spring onions, chilli and coriander leaves among bowls, and ladle in the hot steaming soup. Serve straight away.

Egg drop soup

Serves 4–6

I remember eating this soup at a little local Chinese restaurant quite often when I was younger, and have only recently rediscovered it. It's an incredibly simple soup, made within 15 minutes, and wonderfully good if you need picking up or are feeling under the weather, or just a bit nostalgic.

If you're looking for an accompaniment that admittedly isn't so quick to make, but is mind-blowingly delicious, try the bao buns (see page 257) filled with sticky pork with sesame (see page 205). You won't regret it.

1 litre chicken stock (see page 264), cool or at room temperature

25g cornflour

1 teaspoon finely grated fresh ginger

2 cloves of garlic, finely grated

salt and freshly ground pepper

3 eggs

4 spring onions, thinly sliced at an angle

1–2 teaspoons toasted sesame oil

Place the chicken stock in a saucepan and add the cornflour, ginger and garlic. Whisk the mixture over a medium heat until it comes to the boil, still whisking to ensure that no lumps form. Season to taste with salt and pepper and let it boil for 1 minute, still whisking. Take the pan off the heat for a moment while you break the 3 eggs into a bowl and whisk them well.

Now put the whisk back into the stock in the saucepan, place back over a medium to high heat until simmering, and stir in wide circles with the whisk while you pour the egg in slowly, constantly stirring with the whisk. As the egg hits the soup it will cook in long, thin threads.

Once all the egg has been added, take the soup off the heat and add most of the sliced spring onions and 1 teaspoon of toasted sesame oil. Taste and add more sesame oil if necessary. Serve hot, with the remaining spring onion slices scattered over the top.

SUMMER

Salmorejo with jamón and hard-boiled eggs

Serves 6

A thicker, creamier soup than gazpacho, salmorejo hails from Córdoba in southern Spain's Andalucia region, and is traditionally topped with chopped hard-boiled eggs, jamón serrano and sometimes a little tinned tuna.

Traditionally the tomatoes are peeled for this recipe, but I find that if I'm using really good ripe red tomatoes there's no need to peel them.

800g ripe red tomatoes

100g white bread, slightly stale if possible

1 clove of garlic, crushed or finely grated

100ml extra virgin olive oil

1–2 tablespoons sherry vinegar

salt and freshly ground pepper

a pinch of sugar

To serve

2 eggs

75g serrano ham

a drizzle of extra virgin olive oil

a few flat-leaf parsley leaves

Cut the tomatoes into quarters, remove and discard the cores, and place in a blender. Cut the crusts from the bread and discard, then break the bread into pieces and tip in with the tomatoes. Add the garlic, extra virgin olive oil and 1 tablespoon of sherry vinegar. Season with salt and pepper, then blend until almost smooth.

Taste, adding more vinegar and a pinch of sugar if necessary. Place in the fridge to chill.

While the soup is chilling, place the eggs in boiling water and cook, steadily boiling for 10 minutes, then drain and place in cold water. Peel the eggs, then chop into small pieces.

Cut the serrano ham (the jamón) into thin slivers.

Serve the chilled soup in bowls, with a generous scattering of chopped hard-boiled egg and slivers of serrano ham over the top of each. Drizzle with a few drops of extra virgin olive oil and finish with flat-leaf parsley leaves.

Summer – **soup** broth bread

Roasted red pepper and basil soup with tapenade toasts

Serves 4–6

A super-quick soup, made with store-cupboard favourites, this, if served with garlic-free pesto and tapenade, contains no allium, which will please my wonderful friend and agent greatly, as she can't eat them. This one's for you, Jenny!

2 large red peppers
a drizzle of extra virgin olive oil
2 x 400g tins of plum tomatoes, chopped
2 teaspoons sugar
600ml vegetable or chicken stock (see pages 277, 264)
salt and freshly ground pepper
100ml cream (regular or double), plus a little more for serving (optional)

To serve
6 slices of sourdough or baguette
2 tablespoons extra virgin olive oil
2–3 tablespoons tapenade (see page 194)
1 tablespoon basil pesto (see page 196)

First, roast the peppers. Preheat the oven to 250°C/230°C fan/gas 9. Put some olive oil in your hands and rub all over the skin of the peppers until they're glistening. Place the peppers in a roasting tray and cook in the preheated oven for 25–30 minutes, until the skins are blistered and blackened in patches and the peppers feel soft when you press them with your finger.

Take the peppers out of the oven, place them in a bowl, and either cover tightly with clingfilm or pop a plate over the bowl to make a lid for about 20 minutes (this will make them much easier to peel).

Now peel the skin off the peppers, removing the stalks and all the seeds. Do not wash the peppers or you will lose the precious sweet juices, but you may find that it helps to dip your hands in water every so often to remove the seeds.

While the peppers are roasting, place the chopped tomatoes in a saucepan with the sugar. Bring to the boil, then lower the heat and cook, covered with the lid, for 15 minutes. Add the peeled, roasted peppers and the stock, then bring to the boil and cook for 3 minutes. Season with salt and pepper.

▶

Take the pan off the heat, add the cream, and blend the soup well. Taste for seasoning – this soup does rely on the caster sugar and a few good pinches of salt to balance the tomatoes and peppers.

Toast the bread in a toaster or on a grill pan, then drizzle it with a little olive oil and spread the tapenade on one side.

To serve, reheat the soup and pour into warm bowls. Drizzle with the basil pesto and add a small drizzle of cream, if you wish. Serve with the tapenade toasts.

 notes *Roasted peppers will keep, covered with a layer of olive oil, in your fridge for about 10 days. It's worth roasting some extra, while you have the oven on, to use for a soup or salad another time.*

If you want to buy roasted peppers, use 200g of roasted and peeled peppers for this recipe.

Vichyssoise

It's thought that this classic chilled soup made from leeks, potatoes, stock and cream was created in the early 1900s by a French chef at New York's Ritz-Carlton hotel. Casting about one day for a new soup to put on the menu, he remembered how, on warm mornings, his *maman* used to add cold milk to soup to cool it down. Inspired by this, he added cream and a sprinkle of chives to a leek and potato soup, *et voilà*, Vichyssoise was born. He named it after Vichy, the famous town close to his home, as a tribute to the fine cooking of the region.

 (GF)

50g butter

2 large leeks, base trimmed and all green tops removed (use for stock) (you should have 250g when trimmed), chopped

250g diced potatoes

100g chopped onions

salt and freshly ground pepper (white pepper if you wish)

600ml chicken stock (see page 264)

300ml milk

300ml cream (regular or double)

2 teaspoons finely chopped chives (see note)

Put the butter into a saucepan over a medium to high heat. Allow it to melt and foam, then add the chopped leeks, potatoes and onions. Season with salt and pepper and cover with a butter wrapper or a piece of parchment paper and the saucepan lid. Turn the heat down to very low and cook slowly, stirring every few minutes, for about 10 minutes, until the vegetables are tender.

Add the stock and the milk, season again, and turn the heat up to high. Boil for 1 minute, then remove from the heat and blend until smooth.

Pour the soup into a wide bowl and allow it to cool completely. Place in the fridge until you're ready to finish the soup.

Place the chilled, blended soup in the blender once more, then add the cream and blend until it is smooth and silky. If the potatoes are waxy, you might need a little extra cream.

To serve, pour the soup into small bowls, chilled if you wish, and sprinkle with finely chopped chives.

 note *If the chives that you're using are wet, place them on kitchen paper and pat them dry, then chop them very finely. That way they'll chop more easily and they'll scatter perfectly.*

Beetroot and dill gazpacho

Serves 4–6

This deliciously refreshing chilled soup can be served in bowls as a starter or from shot glasses as a canapé. If you can't find fresh beetroot, you can use boiled beetroot (sometimes available vacuum-packed), though don't be tempted to use pickled beetroot, as it will be too strong. Coriander also works instead of the dill.

(V) (GF)

4 medium beetroots (300g when raw)

50g chopped red onion

1 clove of garlic, crushed or finely grated

200g cucumber, chopped into chunks

2 tablespoons sherry vinegar, or balsamic or red wine vinegar

225ml vegetable or chicken stock (see pages 277, 264)

250ml natural yoghurt

½ tablespoon chopped dill

salt and freshly ground pepper

For the garnish

3cm chunk of cucumber

a couple of teaspoons crème fraîche

½ an avocado, peeled, stoned and finely diced

a drizzle of extra virgin olive oil

a few small sprigs of dill

Scrub the beetroot clean and place them in a saucepan of cold water with a pinch of salt. Bring to the boil and cook for about 30–45 minutes. You can tell when they're cooked by pushing a piece of the skin, and if it comes away from the flesh, it's ready. Drain the beetroot and allow to cool, then use your hands to peel the skin off the beetroot and discard (wear gloves if you want to prevent your fingers going pink!).

Chop the beetroot flesh and place in a blender with the red onion, garlic and cucumber. Add the vinegar, stock, yoghurt and chopped dill, and season with salt and pepper. Blend until smooth, then taste for seasoning, adding more salt, pepper, vinegar or dill if necessary. Place in the fridge to chill.

For the garnish, cut the cucumber in half lengthwise, scoop out the seeds with a teaspoon and dice the cucumber finely. Divide the gazpacho among bowls and very carefully place small blobs of crème fraîche over the top. Scatter with the cucumber and avocado dice, drizzle with a few very small drops of extra virgin olive oil, decorate with small dill sprigs, and serve.

note *If your beetroot still has its stalks and leaves, cut off all but about 1cm of the stalks.*

Nordic salmon and dill soup

Serves 4–6

A very quick soup to make, this is a light chowder with lots of dill. If you wish you can use half smoked and half fresh salmon, and feel free to replace the dill with chives, fennel or parsley.

(GF)

350g fresh salmon, with the skin still attached

1 litre fish or chicken stock (see pages 272, 264)

25g butter

2 leeks, base trimmed and dark green tops removed (see note), halved

lengthwise and sliced across into pieces 5mm thick

2 large potatoes, peeled and cut into 6–8mm dice

salt and freshly ground pepper

100ml cream (regular or double)

2 tablespoons chopped dill, plus a little more for serving

Using a sharp, flexible-bladed knife, slice the salmon flesh off the skin, all in one piece. Put the salmon skin into a saucepan with the stock and place on a high heat. Bring to the boil, then turn the heat down and simmer the stock, covered with a lid, for 10 minutes, to get every bit of goodness and flavour from the salmon skin. If the salmon skin has already been removed, and you don't have it, then omit this step.

Place the butter in another saucepan over a medium to high heat and allow it to melt. Add the leeks and potatoes and season with salt and pepper. Turn the heat down to low, then cover with a butter wrapper or a piece of parchment paper and the saucepan lid, and cook slowly for 8–10 minutes, stirring once or twice during cooking to prevent the vegetables sticking, until the potatoes are almost cooked.

While the potatoes and leeks are cooking, cut the salmon into 1.5cm chunks.

Strain the stock over the vegetables in the saucepan and turn the heat up to high. Once it comes to the boil, add the salmon and the cream and simmer the soup for 4–6 minutes, until the salmon is just cooked. The potatoes should be fully cooked at this stage. Add the chopped dill and season to taste.

Serve with a little more dill scattered over the top.

note *You can use the light green tops of the leeks for this soup, so just remove the dark green tops.*

Lobster, crab or prawn bisque

Serves 4–6

Simple to put together, but decidedly decadent, a bisque is a smooth, rich shellfish soup that is one of my very favourites. Making a bisque out of leftover shellfish heads and shells is a win-win situation; you get double value from your fish. You'll need to use something like a hammer or a rolling pin to crush the heads and shells – they have so much flavour and goodness to give. This bisque is delicious served with prawn ravioli (see page 208).

25g butter

150g chopped shallots

2 cloves of garlic, crushed or finely grated

salt and freshly ground pepper

450g heads, claws, tail shells of prawns, langoustines, lobster or shrimps

2 x 400g tins of plum tomatoes, chopped, or 800g ripe tomatoes, chopped

400ml fish or chicken stock (see pages 272, 264)

1 teaspoon sugar

200ml cream (regular or double)

2 tablespoons brandy

1 tablespoon chopped parsley

Place the butter in a saucepan on a medium heat and when foaming, add the shallots and garlic. Season with salt and pepper, then cover with a butter wrapper or a piece of parchment paper and the lid. Turn the heat down to low and cook gently for about 8–10 minutes, stirring every few minutes to prevent the shallots and garlic sticking and burning.

While the shallots are cooking, use a hammer or rolling pin to crush and bash the heads and shells into smaller pieces. They don't need to be very small, but the more broken up they are, the more flavour you'll extract.

Once the shallots have softened, add the bashed heads and shells to the pan, turn the heat up, and cook uncovered, stirring regularly, for about 6–8 minutes, until you can smell the shells slightly toasting and see them turning light golden in colour.

Add the tomatoes, fish stock or chicken stock and sugar, then cover and cook over a medium to low heat, stirring regularly, for 15 minutes, until the tomatoes have softened completely. Pour into a liquidizer or food processor and whiz for a few minutes to break up the shells (see notes).

Pour through a fine sieve into a clean saucepan and warm through on a medium heat. Add the cream and brandy and season to taste – you may need a pinch more sugar if using tinned tomatoes. Sprinkle with parsley and serve.

The bisque can be made and stored in the fridge for up to 24 hours. It can also be frozen for up to 3 months.

notes *If, for whatever reason, you want to leave the brandy out of the bisque, you can. It'll taste slightly different but it will still be delicious.*

If you're making lobster bisque, where the shells are a bit harder than those of prawns or shrimps, use a mouli-legumes instead of a blender, unless you have a blender with a strong blade, like a Vitamix or Thermomix.

If the bisque is a bit gritty from the shells, it's a good idea to pour it through the sieve a second time.

You can also make crab bisque in this way, but you'll need to use a mouli-legumes instead of a blender. Make sure to remove the lungs (sometimes called dead man's fingers), the feathery cones lining the side of the body. They're not toxic but they don't taste good.

Aubergine and harissa soup with chickpeas

Serves 4–6

Aubergines take on Middle Eastern flavours so well, and in this soup it's harissa, the North African spicy paste, that gives plenty of oomph and kick. For the best flavour, I love to toast and grind whole cumin seeds from scratch, rather than using ready-ground ones. Just toss them in a dry frying pan over a high heat for 2–3 minutes until they turn a few shades darker and become aromatic. Tip them out of the pan and grind using a pestle and mortar, or in a spice grinder.

2 tablespoons extra virgin olive oil

1 large onion, finely chopped

1 large clove of garlic, finely chopped

salt and freshly ground pepper

2 tablespoons harissa paste (see page 194)

2 teaspoons toasted and ground cumin seeds (see above)

1 large aubergine (350g in weight), cut into 1cm cubes

1 x 400g tin of chickpeas (or use dried, see note)

1 x 400g tin of plum tomatoes, chopped, or 400g ripe tomatoes, peeled (see note, page 76) and chopped

600ml vegetable or chicken stock (see pages 277, 264), or 600ml of the chickpea cooking water

1 teaspoon sugar

3 tablespoons coriander leaves

1–2 tablespoons lemon juice

Put the olive oil into a saucepan over a medium heat. Add the chopped onion and garlic and season with salt and pepper. Turn the heat down to low and cook, covered, very gently for 8–10 minutes, until the onions are tender.

Add the harissa paste and the cumin and stir over a high heat for a minute, then tip in the aubergine pieces and stir to coat them with the harissa and onions. Now add the chickpeas, tomatoes and stock, season with salt, pepper and the sugar, then bring to the boil and cook for 20–25 minutes, until the aubergine is completely tender.

Chop the coriander leaves, and the fine stalks at the top, then add to the soup and season to taste with salt, pepper, lemon juice and, if necessary, another small pinch of sugar. Serve in deep warm bowls straight away, or reheat when needed.

 note *You can use 125g dried chickpeas instead of a 400g tin. Pre-soak in plenty of cold water for 5 hours or overnight, then drain and place in a saucepan with fresh cold water to cover. Bring to the boil over a high heat, then lower to a simmer and cook for approximately 45 minutes, until tender.*

Leek and fennel soup with smoked salmon soldiers

Serves 4

This delicious blended soup has a smooth, silky richness, but if you'd prefer it a little less rich, you can use half milk and half cream, or even all milk instead of the cream. The smoked salmon soldiers bring their own burst of flavour for a lovely little lunch or supper.

1 large fennel bulb

2 medium leeks

25g butter

1 large potato, peeled and diced
   (150g when peeled)

salt and freshly ground pepper

500ml chicken or vegetable stock
   (see pages 264, 277)

100ml cream (regular or double)

For the smoked salmon soldiers

4 slices of white or sourdough bread

softened butter

4 slices of smoked salmon

squeeze of lemon juice

freshly ground black pepper

Cut the feathery fronds from the fennel bulb and reserve for later. Trim off the top stalks and the base. Also trim the leeks, removing their green tops and their bases. Discard all the trimmings or put into your stockpot if you have one (see page 264). Cut the trimmed fennel and the leeks into dice.

Melt the butter in a saucepan over a medium heat, then add the fennel and leeks, and the chopped potato. Stir and season with salt and pepper, then cover with a leftover butter wrapper, butter side down, or a piece of parchment paper. Turn the heat down to low, cover with the lid and cook for 10 minutes, until the vegetables are just tender. Remove the lid and stir every so often during cooking, so the veg don't stick and burn.

Add the stock and turn the heat up to high. Cook for a couple of minutes, until the vegetables are completely tender. Add the cream and blend until smooth, then taste for seasoning. Serve straight away or reheat gently, scattering the reserved fennel fronds over the top of the soup.

To make the smoked salmon soldiers, preheat the grill to high. Toast the pieces of bread on both sides, then spread with softened butter and top with slices of smoked salmon. Pop back under the grill for a minute, until the salmon is pale pink and opaque. Squeeze a little lemon juice over the top and sprinkle with some black pepper. Cut into fingers and serve with the hot soup.

Tomato, coconut and coriander soup

Serves 6

The fresh acidity of tomatoes adores the smooth silkiness of coconut milk, and for an extra Asian flavour I add lots of chopped fresh coriander. Tinned tomatoes and coconut milk are two of my must-have store-cupboard ingredients. This is a super-speedy soup to make, and happily, it can also be frozen.

(V)

(GF)

1 tablespoon coconut oil

1 onion, finely chopped

salt, freshly ground pepper and sugar

2 x 400g tins of plum tomatoes, chopped, or 800g fresh tomatoes, peeled (see note) and chopped

1 x 400ml tin of coconut milk

250ml vegetable or chicken stock (see pages 277, 264)

2 tablespoons chopped coriander (the leaves and the tender stalks at the top)

For the garnish

1–2 tablespoons crème fraîche

a few coriander leaves

Place a saucepan on a medium heat and add the coconut oil. Allow to melt, then tip in the chopped onion and season with salt and pepper. Turn the heat down to low, then cover the onions with a butter wrapper or a piece of parchment paper and a lid, and cook gently, stirring from time to time, for 10 minutes, until soft but not coloured.

Add the tomatoes (plus any juice), the coconut milk and the vegetable or chicken stock, and season with salt, pepper and a few pinches of sugar. Bring to the boil, then reduce the heat and simmer for 5 minutes, until the tomatoes are tasting mellow and cooked.

Add the chopped coriander and blend well. Season to taste and serve immediately, or reheat when needed.

To serve, spoon a few small blobs of crème fraîche on to each bowl of hot soup and finish with a few coriander leaves.

note *To peel fresh tomatoes, cut an X through the skin, then put them into a bowl. Cover them with boiling water and leave them for 10–15 seconds, until the skins are loose and will peel off easily.*

Roasted tomato and basil soup with basil oil

Serves 4–6

A seasonal match made in heaven, the combination of tomato and basil makes this a perfect summer recipe. I love the speediness of this soup, and the basil oil, once made, will keep in the fridge for up to a month, for adding a sunny flavour to countless other soups, pastas, meat and fish dishes.

900g ripe tomatoes (about 8 large tomatoes), halved

1 red onion, peeled and thickly sliced

3 large cloves of garlic, peeled

2 sprigs of basil

2 tablespoons extra virgin olive oil

1 tablespoon balsamic vinegar

sea salt and freshly ground pepper

1 teaspoon caster sugar

600ml vegetable or chicken stock (see pages 277, 264)

50ml cream (regular or double)

50ml basil oil (see page 200)

basil leaves, to serve

Preheat the oven to 220°C/200°C fan/gas 7.

Arrange the tomato halves, cut side up, in a single layer on a baking tray and tuck the onion, garlic and basil sprigs in between them. Drizzle over the olive oil and balsamic vinegar and season well with salt and pepper and the sugar. Roast in the oven for 25–30 minutes, or until the tomatoes have softened and are a little blistered around the edges.

Once cooked, remove the basil stalks (the leaves can stay with the tomatoes) and tip the entire contents of the baking tray, including any juices, into a blender. Add the stock and blend until smooth, then pour into a saucepan. Alternatively, tip the cooked tomatoes into the saucepan, pour in the stock and purée using a hand-held blender. If you're using a blender that's not very powerful, it's worth pouring the soup through a sieve after blending, so that it's lovely and smooth.

Bring the soup to the boil, add the cream, then reduce the heat and simmer to heat through.

Ladle the soup into warm bowls and drizzle just a teaspoon or two of basil oil over each. Garnish with a few basil leaves.

Soupe au pistou

Serves 8–10

This classic comforting soup hails from Provence and contains lots of different vegetables, but if I don't have some of them I just make do and use more of the others. I've been known to go off-piste with this soup and add spicy sausage such as kabanossi or chorizo, and if I make it in wintertime I'll use good tinned plum tomatoes instead of fresh (a 400g tin with all the juices works for this quantity).

There are so many different recipes for soupe au pistou, and like its Italian cousin minestrone, the vegetables put in will depend on what's in season, so feel free to be led by nature.

Any broken pasta can be used, or small shapes like macaroni or orzo, or even rice. Sometimes Gruyère cheese is used instead of Parmesan, and this is also delicious.

Meanwhile, pistou is a fantastically garlicky French cousin of pesto. It contains no nuts and lots of garlic and cheese, and it's so good for drizzling over this soup and many others. If you wish, however, you could use a pesto, such as wild garlic, parsley or kale (see pages 199, 198), if you have one in the fridge.

75g dried haricot or borlotti beans, soaked overnight in plenty of cold water, then drained

2.25 litres chicken stock (see page 264)

salt and freshly ground pepper

3 tablespoons extra virgin olive oil, plus extra for drizzling

1 large onion, finely chopped

3 medium carrots, cut into 5mm dice

2 medium leeks, halved lengthwise and cut into 5mm thin slices

3 small white turnips, peeled and cut into 5mm dice

2 celery stalks, cut into 5mm dice (peel outer stalks to remove tough exterior)

2 large waxy potatoes, peeled and cut into 5mm dice

2 medium courgettes, cut into 5mm dice

5 ripe tomatoes, peeled (see note, page 76) and chopped

250g French beans, cut into 1cm lengths at an angle

50g vermicelli pasta

a few pinches of sugar

50g finely grated Parmesan cheese, to serve

For the pistou

5 large cloves of garlic, crushed or finely grated

15g basil leaves

75ml extra virgin olive oil

50g finely grated Parmesan cheese

▸

Cover the beans with the chicken stock, bring to the boil and cook until tender, adding some salt towards the end of the cooking time. When the beans are cooked, do not drain them but set them aside in the cooking liquid, as this is the stock for the soup.

While the beans are cooking, heat the olive oil in a large saucepan and add the chopped onions, carrots, leeks, turnip and celery. Season with salt and pepper and turn the heat down to low. Cook, covered with the lid, for 6–8 minutes, until the vegetables are starting to soften, then add the potatoes, courgettes, tomatoes, French beans and the broken vermicelli.

Season with salt, freshly ground pepper and a few good pinches of sugar to balance the acidity of the tomatoes, then add the cooked beans and all their cooking liquid. Cover and simmer for about 30 minutes, until everything is tender and delicious. If the mixture has been boiling too ferociously, you might need to add another bit of chicken stock or water to thin it out slightly. Taste for seasoning once more and take off the heat.

Meanwhile, make the pistou. Place the garlic in a food processor, then add the basil and blend the two together with a little olive oil. Mix in the grated Parmesan, then add the rest of the olive oil, and season to taste.

To serve, stir some of the pistou into the hot soup just before serving, and scatter some more grated Parmesan generously over the top. Finish with a drizzle of extra virgin olive oil, *et voilà*.

Serve with crusty bread, and if you wish with some more pistou and grated cheese on the side.

Pea and coriander soup

Serves 4–6

We make this soup at Ballymaloe Cookery School. It's such a good, fast recipe and it has to be one of my favourites. I always have a bag of peas in the freezer, and if you feel like leaving out the garlic and chilli, and replacing the coriander with mint, that's great too. If I'm in a big rush and have spring onions to hand, I'll chop six of those instead of the regular onion, and cook them for just 4 minutes.

(V)
(GF)

25g butter
150g finely chopped onion
2 cloves of garlic, chopped
½–1 green chilli, deseeded
and chopped
salt and freshly ground pepper

850ml vegetable or chicken stock
(see pages 277, 264)
450g peas (I use good frozen peas)
2 tablespoons chopped coriander,
plus a few whole leaves for garnish
1–2 tablespoons of crème fraîche
(optional)

Melt the butter in a saucepan on a medium heat until foaming, then add the onion, garlic and chilli and season with salt and pepper. Cover with a butter wrapper or a piece of parchment paper, put on the lid, and cook over a low heat for 8–10 minutes, until the onions are tender, stirring every so often.

Add the stock, then turn up the heat to high and bring to the boil. Now add the peas and cook very rapidly, making sure to remove the lid as soon as the stock comes back to the boil (this keeps the peas' fresh green colour intact), for only 1 or 2 minutes, or until the peas are cooked.

As soon as the peas are cooked, add the chopped coriander and immediately liquidize. Check the seasoning and serve. If you wish you can dollop a few small blobs of crème fraîche over the top, and perhaps add a few coriander leaves.

notes

Like many soups, this freezes really well.

Avoid prolonged boiling and simmering of this soup, to retain the fresh green colour.

For a dairy-free version, replace the butter with 2 tablespoons of extra virgin olive oil.

If you're using fresh podded peas, these will take about 3–4 minutes to cook.

Mexican chilaquiles soup

Serves 4–6

This is my rather unorthodox but delicious soupy take on one of my favourite Mexican breakfast dishes, chilaquiles. It's a traditional dish of day-old tortillas that are fried and drenched in a red or green chilli sauce and topped with onions, sour cream and queso fresco, the local crumbly cheese, for which I have substituted feta. A taste of this transports me right back to a café on the Zócalo, the main square in Oaxaca, southern Mexico, where I had shredded chicken in mine, and refried beans and avocado were served with it too.

I love to use pickled jalapeños in this soup, but if you can't find a jar, you can use fresh green chillies or the slightly sweeter red jalapeños. These are the chillies used in a chilaquiles, as they were always originally grown in Mexico, but feel free to replace them with another moderately mild chilli if you can't get jalapeños.

800g fresh ripe tomatoes, quartered, or 2 x 400g tins of plum tomatoes

100g roughly chopped red onions

2 large cloves of garlic

1–2 pickled or fresh jalapeño chillies, sliced

600ml chicken or vegetable stock (see pages 264, 277)

2 handfuls of coriander stalks

salt and freshly ground pepper

1 teaspoon sugar

200g raw chicken breast, sliced as thinly as you can manage (see note)

To serve

4–6 corn tortillas

olive oil, for frying

1 small ripe avocado, peeled, stoned and sliced

2 tablespoons crème fraîche

50g feta cheese

1 jalapeño chilli, finely sliced

4–6 lime wedges

Place the tomatoes in a blender with the onion, garlic, chilli and stock. Take the leaves off the coriander stalks, set the leaves aside for serving, and add the stalks, roughly chopped, to the blender. Blend until smooth, then season with salt, pepper and the sugar and place in a saucepan.

Bring to the boil, then cook, uncovered, over a medium heat for 5 minutes. Add the sliced raw chicken and continue to cook for another 10 minutes. Season to taste with more salt, pepper and sugar, if necessary.

▶

Cut the corn tortillas into wedges. Heat some olive oil in a frying pan – the oil should be at least 2cm deep. When it's hot, drop the wedges into it and cook until they're a couple of shades darker and starting to get crisp. Drain on kitchen paper.

Pour the soup into warm bowls and top each with some of the crisp tortilla wedges, a few slices of avocado, about 4 or 5 half-teaspoon blobs of crème fraîche, a crumbling of feta cheese, some chilli slices and the reserved coriander leaves. Finish with a juicy wedge of lime, and serve.

notes *This soup is also delicious made without the chicken, and using a vegetable stock, for a meat-free version.*

This is a great way to use up leftover roast chicken. Just shred it very finely and add it to the soup 1 minute before you finish cooking.

Shellfish chowder with tomatoes and cream

Serves 4–6

More than just a starter, a chowder is often a meal in a bowl, and this wonderfully hearty version is creamy and luxurious too. Seek out a good selection of shellfish if you can, and cook it just before eating for the very best result.

15g butter
1 large onion, finely chopped
1 large celery stalk
salt and freshly ground pepper
1 large clove of garlic, finely chopped
400g ripe red tomatoes, peeled (see note, page 76) and chopped, or 1 x 400g tin of plum tomatoes, chopped
a large pinch of sugar
75ml dry white wine
750ml fish or chicken stock (see pages 272, 264)

300g filleted and skinned raw fish, such as round white fish and salmon
100g raw prawns, shrimps or scallops, or a mixture
1kg raw mussels and cockles or clams, in their shells
150ml cream (regular or double)
juice of ½–1 lemon
2 teaspoons chopped chives
1 teaspoon chopped fennel
1 tablespoon chopped parsley

Put the butter into a large saucepan over a medium heat and allow to melt. Add the chopped onion and celery and season with salt and pepper. Cover with a leftover butter wrapper or a piece of parchment paper and the saucepan lid, and turn the heat down to low. Cook for 8–10 minutes, stirring once or twice, until the onions and celery are tender. Add the garlic and cook for another couple of minutes, still covered.

Now remove the lid and paper, turn the heat up to medium-high, and add the tomatoes with a good pinch of sugar and the white wine. Cook the mixture, uncovered, over a low heat for about 10–15 minutes, until the tomatoes have softened completely, then add the stock and simmer again for 5 minutes.

Meanwhile, prepare the seafood. Cut the filleted and skinned fish into 1–2cm chunks. If using prawns, cut them in half if they're large, and cut the scallops into halves or quarters. If the shrimps are small, leave them whole, and if they're large, cut them in half. Scrub the mussels and cockles or clams in a sink full of cold

▶

water, discarding any that are open and do not close when you tap the shell on the worktop.

You can prepare the chowder in advance up to this point if you wish, in which case, place the seafood in the fridge. Once the chowder base with the tomatoes and stock has cooled, put that into the fridge too.

About 15–20 minutes before you're ready to eat, reheat the tomato and stock base and bring to a simmer. Taste it for seasoning, adding a little more salt, sugar and pepper if necessary. Add all the seafood and gently cover it with the tomato mixture, then cover with the lid until the mixture comes back to a simmer. Continue to cook, covered, for about 6–8 minutes, until the fish is all cooked and the mussel and cockle or clam shells are wide open. Discard any that haven't opened.

Add the cream, stirring gently to mix it in so as not to break up the fish. Now add the lemon juice to season, and the chopped chives, fennel and most of the parsley.

Serve in deep, warm bowls, with a final scattering of chopped parsley over the top.

Courgette and basil soup with aïoli croutons

Serves 4–6

Courgettes make a fabulous soup, whether in a chunky broth, or a creamy blended one like this recipe here. The aïoli croutons add a lovely punchy crunch to this delicious late summer soup.

2 tablespoons extra virgin olive oil

1 large onion (200g), chopped

1 large clove of garlic, chopped

salt and freshly ground pepper

2 courgettes (350g in weight altogether), diced

800ml vegetable or chicken stock (see pages 277, 264)

8 large basil leaves

30g finely grated hard cheese, e.g. Parmesan or vegetarian option

100ml cream (regular or double)

For the aïoli croutons

2–3 slices of delicious white bread or sourdough

2 tablespoons extra virgin olive oil

2 tablespoons aïoli (see page 195)

Place the olive oil in a saucepan over a medium heat. Add the chopped onion and garlic, season with salt and pepper, then cover with a butter wrapper or a piece of parchment paper. Put the saucepan lid on and reduce the heat to low, then cook gently for about 10 minutes, until the onions are tender. Add the courgettes, then cover again and cook for another 3–4 minutes, until the courgettes are just tender.

Now add the stock, bring the mixture to the boil over a high heat and boil for 1 minute. Take off the heat, add the basil leaves, grated cheese and cream, and blend until smooth. Season to taste.

Preheat the grill to high. Slice the crusts from the bread and discard. Cut the bread into 3cm chunks and toss them in a bowl with the olive oil. Tip on to a baking tray, spreading the croutons out in a single layer, and place under the grill for 2–3 minutes, turning them and giving the tray a shake halfway through, until the croutons are golden brown.

Allow to cool slightly, then place a small dollop of aïoli on each crouton and place on top of each bowl of hot soup.

Tomato and basil water

Far more delicious than it sounds, this clear soup is the essence of tomatoes, the ultimate flavour of summer. Enjoy it chilled as tomato water, or hot as tomato consommé (see variation). The more delicious the tomatoes, the better this will taste. If the tomatoes are lacking slightly in flavour, you may need to tweak the seasoning a little bit more.

1.35kg ripe red tomatoes

75g shallots or red onion

2 cloves of garlic, peeled

a handful of basil leaves (about 15g)

1½ tablespoons white wine vinegar

1½ teaspoons sugar

½ teaspoon salt

freshly ground black pepper

a few basil leaves, to serve

Chop the tomatoes roughly and place in a blender. Cut the shallot or red onion, whichever you're using, into chunks, and add to the blender with the garlic, basil, vinegar, sugar and salt. Add a pinch of black pepper and blend the mixture until almost fine.

Place a large sieve over a bowl, with a piece of muslin (see note) that's larger than the sieve sitting in it.

Pour the tomato mixture into the sieve, then tie the piece of muslin at the top with string. You can sit the muslin in the sieve or you can tie it to a hook so that it drips into the bowl, with no sieve needed. It will drip slightly faster if it's hanging, but it's not essential.

After a few hours, or overnight, you should have about 750ml of tomato water, and the tomato pulp should feel quite dry.

Taste the tomato water, adding a drizzle more vinegar if it needs it, or salt and pepper. Serve chilled in small glasses or bowls, with a basil leaf floating on top of each.

variation   tomato consommé: *Heat the tomato water until steaming and serve in small bowls, with a basil leaf floating on top of each.*

note   *If you don't have any muslin, you can just use a large fine sieve, but don't be tempted to push the mixture through the sieve or the tomato water will be cloudy.*

Watermelon, mint and gin soup shots

Makes 6–8 shots

Fun and vibrant, these fruity little shots make a lovely summery appetizer or aperitif. Served chilled on a warm day.

25ml caster sugar

300g watermelon, peel removed (weight after deseeding and peeling)

2 tablespoons chopped mint

100ml gin

1 tablespoon lime juice

1 tablespoon lemon juice

Place the caster sugar in a bowl and pour in 25ml of boiling water. Stir to dissolve the sugar. Allow to cool. Place a piece of muslin or a single thin sheet of kitchen paper in a sieve sitting over a bowl.

Pour the sugar syrup into a blender with the watermelon, the mint, the gin and the lime and lemon juice. Blend until smooth, then pour into the sieve and allow to drip through into the bowl. Taste and add a little more lime juice if necessary.

Serve chilled, in shot glasses.

note   *To deseed a watermelon, cut it into slices, then, using your hands, gently break each slice along the vein of seeds, and scrape them out using the tip of a knife.*

Chilled cucumber and tarragon soup

Serves 4–6

A deliciously refreshing soup, perfect for a hot summer's day. If I feel like a change, or just don't have any tarragon, fresh mint, dill or coriander also work really well in this great little starter.

1 cucumber (approximately 400g in weight), chopped into chunks

1 shallot (25g), cut into quarters

1 clove of garlic, chopped

1 tablespoon tarragon leaves

200ml natural yoghurt

juice of ½–1 lemon

2 tablespoons cream (regular or double)

salt and freshly ground pepper

To serve

2 teaspoons natural yoghurt

a drizzle of extra virgin olive oil

Place the cucumber, shallot and garlic in a blender with the tarragon, yoghurt, the juice of ½ the lemon and the cream. Add some salt and pepper and blend until smooth.

Season again to taste, adding more lemon juice if necessary.

Served chilled, in small bowls, with little blobs of yoghurt and a drizzle of extra virgin olive oil over the top.

Watermelon gazpacho

I adore this simple summer soup – it's just perfect for a hot day. The salty feta works so well with the sweet juicy watermelon. For an extra crunch, scatter some toasted pumpkin seeds on top when serving, if you wish.

625g watermelon, peel removed and cut into pieces (weight after deseeding and peeling)

200g cucumber, chopped into chunks

200g ripe red tomatoes

25g red onion, chopped

2 tablespoons extra virgin olive oil

1 tablespoon red wine vinegar

sea salt

To serve

50g feta cheese

a drizzle of extra virgin olive oil

Place the watermelon pieces in a blender. Cut out the cores from the tomatoes, then cut the tomatoes into chunks and add to the blender with the cucumber. Add the red onion, olive oil, red wine vinegar and a pinch of sea salt. Blend well, then taste for seasoning.

Place the gazpacho in the fridge to chill until serving. It can be made a day in advance if you wish.

To serve, pour the cold gazpacho into bowls, crumble over the feta cheese and drizzle a few drops of extra virgin olive oil over the top.

note   *See note on page 94 on deseeding a watermelon.*

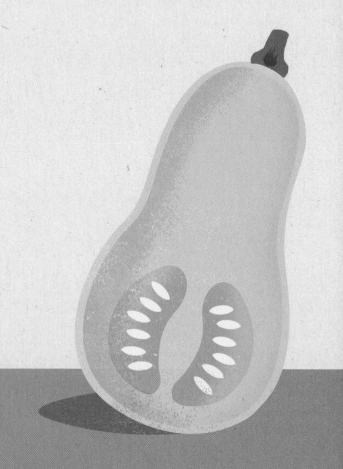

AUTUMN

Ginger and bok choy broth with poached eggs

Serves 4–6

This quick-to-make and super-nourishing soup is restorative yet wonderfully light. If I'm making it in springtime, I'll sometimes replace the bok choy with wild garlic leaves, about 2 large handfuls in total. If using large bok choy heads, then just one will do, cut crossways into 1cm-thick slices. For a gluten-free broth, you can use tamari in place of the soy sauce.

GF

1 tablespoon toasted sesame oil (see note)

3cm piece of fresh ginger, cut into thin slices

2–3 cloves of garlic, cut into thin slices

1 litre chicken stock or Asian chicken stock (see pages 264, 268)

2 tablespoons soy sauce (see above)

3 small heads of bok choy

4 eggs

3 spring onions, trimmed and sliced very thinly at an angle

Pour the sesame oil into a wide saucepan and place over a medium-high heat until warm. Quickly add the sliced ginger and garlic, and cook, stirring constantly, until the garlic is starting to turn golden around the edges, about 1 minute.

Pour in the chicken stock and soy sauce and bring to the boil. Taste for seasoning and add more soy sauce if you wish.

Meanwhile, trim and discard the ends from the base of the bok choy and cut each head into quarters lengthwise. Add to the boiling broth and cook for 1 minute. While the bok choy is cooking, crack an egg into a teacup or mug with a handle.

Turn down the heat to maintain a simmer and gently pour the egg from the cup on to the surface of the broth – this way you'll be able to lower the eggs into the broth really gently but won't burn your fingers. Repeat with the other eggs, placing them as far apart from each other as possible, preferably not touching. Simmer the broth without stirring until the egg whites are set but the yolks are still runny, about 3–4 minutes.

Serve immediately, giving each person 3 wedges of bok choy in the broth, and one egg, topped with the sliced spring onions.

note   *When buying toasted sesame oil, make sure it only contains sesame oil. If you see 'blended with other oils or vegetable oils', it's not pure.*

French onion soup with Gruyère toasts

Serves 6–8

A famously simple and heartwarming dish made with onions and beef broth, this soup originated in Paris in the 1700s. One of the most loved of all French soups, it still features on the menus of bistros and train station cafés all around France. While not traditional, I love to add garlic, white wine and thyme to my French onion soup, but if you're a purist, feel free to leave them out.

Make sure to cook the onions really slowly and for a very long time, so that they get beautifully and evenly caramelized – the flavour of the soup relies upon this.

1.5kg onions

50g butter

salt and freshly ground pepper

4 cloves of garlic, chopped

1 teaspoon chopped thyme leaves

250ml dry white wine

1.5 litres good homemade beef or chicken stock (or vegetable stock for a vegetarian soup) (see pages 270, 264, 277)

To serve

6 slices of baguette, 1cm thick, toasted

125g grated Gruyère or vegetarian option

Peel the onions and slice thinly. Melt the butter in a large saucepan. Add the onions, season with salt and pepper, stir, and cook on a low heat for 60–70 minutes with the lid off, stirring very frequently. The onions will go from being pale to deep dark golden, but they shouldn't be burnt. I use a wooden spatula to scrape the bottom of the saucepan every 5 or so minutes when the onions really start to caramelize.

A few minutes before the onions are ready, add the chopped garlic. When the onions are deeply caramelized, add the thyme and white wine and cook for a few minutes, then add the stock, season with salt and pepper, and bring to the boil. Turn the heat down low and simmer for 15 minutes, uncovered, then taste and correct the seasoning.

Ladle into deep heatproof bowls, place a slice of toasted baguette on top, and cover the bread generously with grated cheese. Place under a hot preheated grill, or in a hot oven, until the cheese is melted and golden. Serve straight away (but beware, it will all be very hot). It's traditional to finish the soup under the grill like this, so that any stray cheese melts into the soup deliciously, but you can alternatively cook the Gruyère toasts separately under the grill, then place them on top of the soup to serve.

Creamy mushroom soup with mushroom and Parmesan bruschetta

Serves 4–6

A mushroom soup can be nice . . . or it can be excellent! In this delicious version, there's lots of great extra flavour coming from the garlic and the herbs, and a velvety texture from the generous splash of cream. Exotic mushrooms, while optional, will bring an additional earthiness that makes this soup very special. Use good-quality crusty bread and extra virgin olive oil for the bruschetta – it'll be worth it.

3 tablespoons extra virgin olive oil

1 large onion (200g), finely chopped

2 large celery stalks, finely chopped

2 large cloves of garlic, crushed or finely grated

salt and freshly ground pepper

750g mushrooms (I like to include a mix of oyster, chestnut and shiitake mushrooms), thinly sliced

2 teaspoons chopped sage or thyme leaves

1 litre vegetable or chicken stock (see pages 277, 264)

100ml cream (regular or double)

a drizzle of extra virgin olive oil

For the bruschetta

4–6 slices of sourdough or white yeast bread

1 clove of garlic, cut in half

a drizzle of extra virgin olive oil

1 tablespoon chopped parsley

sea salt

a chunk of Parmesan cheese (or vegetarian option) and a cheese slicer

Pour the olive oil into a saucepan over a medium heat and add the onions, celery and garlic. Season with salt and pepper, cover with a butter wrapper or a piece of parchment paper and the saucepan lid, then turn down the heat and cook for about 10 minutes, until the onions and celery are completely softened.

Add the mushrooms to the onion mixture, turn the heat up to high, and cook until the mushrooms are wilted and golden. Stir in the chopped sage or thyme.

Spoon out 4 generous tablespoons of the mushroom mixture and set aside in a small saucepan for the mushroom bruschetta. Now add the stock to the rest of the mushrooms in the larger saucepan and bring to the boil. Simmer for 10 minutes, until the flavours have all mingled. Add the cream and blend the soup until smooth and creamy.

To make the mushroom bruschetta, toast or grill the slices of bread, then rub the cut clove of garlic on just one side of each piece, drizzle with a little olive oil and season. While the bread is toasting or grilling, reheat the mushroom mixture, seasoning it to taste, and add the chopped parsley.

Set aside a few mushroom slices to garnish the soup, and spoon the rest of the sautéd mushrooms over the bruschetta. Shave some Parmesan over the top, and serve the bruschetta alongside a bowl of steaming hot mushroom soup, garnished with the reserved mushroom slices and drizzled with a little extra virgin olive oil.

Game broth with lentils, garlic and parsley

Serves 4–6

This comforting bowl of goodness will warm the cockles of your heart. It's best made using game stock from the bones of roasted pheasant, partridge, guinea fowl, duck or grouse, but if you don't have game stock, or there isn't enough, use chicken, goose or duck stock.

Instead of the chopped parsley, you could use finely chopped wild garlic when in season, or kale, though finely chopped kale will take about 3 minutes to cook once it's gone into the saucepan. The 6 large cloves of garlic may sound like a lot, but when they're cooked slowly in their skins with the lentils, they take on a gloriously sweet flavour.

For the lentils

175g Puy lentils

1 onion, peeled and halved

1 carrot, peeled and halved

6 large whole unpeeled cloves of garlic

1 bouquet garni

500ml game stock (see page 269)

For the broth

3 tablespoons extra virgin olive oil

1 small onion, peeled and very finely chopped

1 small celery stalk, peeled and cut into fine dice

1 small carrot, peeled and cut into fine dice

sea salt and freshly ground pepper

1 litre game stock (see page 269)

2 tablespoons finely chopped parsley

Put the lentils into a saucepan with the onion, carrot, whole garlic cloves and the bouquet garni. Add the 500ml of stock and bring to the boil. Turn the heat down and simmer over a low heat, with the lid on, for 15–20 minutes, until the lentils are tender but still retaining their shape. Keep an eye on the liquid level in the saucepan, making sure the lentils are just covered at all times – if not, add a little water to top it up.

Once the lentils are cooked, remove the carrot, onion and bouquet garni. Do not drain the lentils. Squeeze the garlic cloves out of their skins, then chop finely and stir into the lentils and liquid. Set aside.

To make the soup, while the lentils are cooking, place another saucepan over a medium heat and add the olive oil. Tip in the chopped onions, diced celery and carrot. Season with salt and pepper, cover with a butter wrapper or a piece of parchment paper and the saucepan lid, then turn the heat down to low and cook until the vegetables are just tender, about 10 minutes.

Add the 1 litre of stock and bring to a simmer, cooking for a minute or two until the vegetables are completely tender. Now add the lentils and all the liquid to the pan, along with the chopped parsley. Bring to the boil, then taste and correct the seasoning, if necessary. Ladle into warm bowls to serve.

note   *If you have any scraps of game meat left over, cut them into fine dice and add them to the broth with the lentils.*

Roasted parsnip, garlic and haricot bean soup with sage

Serves 6

This is a supremely smooth and silky soup, topped with deliciously crisp fried sage leaves. The garlic cloves, when roasted in their skins, deliver a sweet but rounded depth that I adore. A perfect soup for a cold blustery day.

(VG)

(GF)

3 medium or 2 large parsnips, peeled and cut into 2cm chunks

1 large onion, peeled and cut into 2cm chunks

6 very large, whole unpeeled cloves of garlic (40g in total)

2 tablespoons extra virgin olive oil

salt and freshly ground pepper

1 x 400g tin of haricot beans (see note)

1 litre vegetable or chicken stock (see pages 277, 264)

1 tablespoon chopped sage

To serve

2 tablespoons extra virgin olive oil

a handful of sage leaves

Preheat the oven to 200°C/180°C fan/gas 6. Place the parsnip and onion chunks in a roasting tray with the whole unpeeled cloves of garlic. Drizzle over the olive oil and toss the vegetables, seasoning with salt and pepper. Spread them out to cover the base of the roasting tray and place in the preheated oven for 35–45 minutes, until the vegetables are tender and a little golden around the edges.

Drain the tin of beans and tip all but a generous tablespoon of beans into the vegetables. Return to the oven for 5 minutes more.

Take the tray out of the oven and tip the beans and vegetables and any delicious juices into a saucepan with the hot stock. Add the 1 tablespoon of chopped sage and blend the soup until smooth and silky. Season to taste.

To serve, pour the hot soup into warm bowls. Put the 2 tablespoons of olive oil into a small frying pan and allow to get hot. Add the sage leaves and fry for 10–15 seconds, until they turn a couple of shades darker and become fragrant. Spoon the sage-flavoured oil and the crispy sage leaves over the soup with the reserved beans, and serve straight away.

note   *If you're cooking dried beans from scratch, you'll need 125g of haricot (or cannellini) beans. Soak in plenty of cold water overnight or for at least 5 hours, then drain, cover with plenty of fresh cold water and boil for 30–40 minutes, until tender.*

Santa Fe soup

Serves 6

This chunky and delicious 'meal-in-a-bowl' gets its inspiration from a soup that my friend and agent Jenny used to enjoy when she lived in New Mexico. It sounds like a massive amount of chillies, but when grilled they lose a lot of their raw heat and you end up with a sweet and almost tropical fruit flavour.

For the salsa

8–10 mild green chillies, such as poblano or the slightly hotter jalapeño chillies

a drizzle of extra virgin olive oil

100g roughly chopped onions

2 cloves of garlic, roughly chopped

4 large ripe red tomatoes

2 tablespoons chopped coriander

salt and a pinch of sugar

For the soup

2 tablespoons extra virgin olive oil

2 onions (275g), finely chopped

salt and freshly ground pepper

2 large cloves of garlic, finely chopped

2 large chicken breasts, cut into 1cm dice

150ml dry sherry

1.25 litres chicken stock (see page 264)

To serve, per person

15g grated Cheddar cheese

a teaspoon of sour cream

a sprinkle of coriander leaves

tortilla chips (see page 190)

First, make the roasted green chilli salsa. Preheat the oven to 250°C/230°C fan/gas 9, or preheat your grill to its highest setting. Rub the outside of the chillies with a little olive oil, then put them on a baking tray and place in the preheated oven or under the grill. Cook them in the oven, turning halfway through, for about 10–15 minutes, until they're deep golden in patches on the outside and slightly collapsed. They'll only take about 5–8 minutes altogether under the grill. The chilli flesh under the skin should be soft and tender.

Transfer the hot chillies into a bowl, cover with a plate and allow to cool. This will trap the steam, which helps the skins to lift easily from the flesh of the chillies. Once the chillies are cool, place them on a chopping board, then peel off and discard the skins and the stems. Cut the chillies in half lengthwise and scrape out and discard the seeds.

Place the chilli flesh in a food processor and blend with the onion and garlic. You might need to add 1 or 2 tablespoons of water if it's getting stuck in the food processor.

Tip the green chilli salsa into a bowl.

Peel the tomatoes (see note, page 76), then chop them into pieces smaller than 1cm. Stir the tomatoes through the green chilli salsa, add the chopped coriander, and season with salt to taste. You might need a pinch of sugar too. Set the salsa aside.

To make the soup, pour the olive oil into a saucepan over a medium heat and add the chopped onions. Season with salt and pepper and turn the heat down to low. Cover with a lid and cook the onions, stirring regularly, until they are soft and slightly golden around the edges, about 10 minutes. Add the chopped garlic after 5 minutes and continue to cook.

Tip the onions and garlic out of the saucepan into a bowl or on to a plate, then place the pan back on the heat, turning it up to high. Add another tablespoon of olive oil and the diced chicken. Cook the chicken on all sides until light golden, about 3 minutes, then tip the onions and garlic back in. Add the sherry and bring to a simmer, cooking it uncovered for 2 minutes, then pour in the stock. Bring to a simmer again and cook for 5 minutes, then add half the salsa and taste the soup. You want an amount of heat that is good for everyone. The remaining salsa is to serve alongside, for people who want an extra kick of chilli. Cook the soup for another 5 minutes, then take off the heat.

Place some grated cheese in the bottom of each bowl and fill with hot soup. Top with a drizzle of green chilli salsa, a teaspoon of sour cream, a few coriander leaves and some tortilla chips.

Carrot, cumin and coriander soup

Serves 4-6

The sweet earthy flavour of carrots goes so well with spices. I love the warm, nutty notes of cumin and coriander, and while you can use ready-ground spices in this recipe, when they're freshly toasted and ground they are fantastically good. If you wish, this soup can be made without dairy. Just use 2–3 tablespoons of extra virgin olive oil in place of the butter and leave out the cream or milk at the end, replacing it with extra stock. As is the case with so many soups, this one freezes very well.

2 teaspoons cumin seeds
2 teaspoons coriander seeds
25g butter
125g chopped onions
150g chopped potatoes
550g carrots, peeled and chopped
salt and freshly ground pepper
1 litre vegetable or chicken stock
(see pages 277, 264)

½ a lemon
150ml cream or milk

To serve
2 tablespoons crème fraîche or
yoghurt
a few coriander leaves
toasted pitta wedges (see page 190)

Put the cumin and coriander seeds into a dry frying pan and cook over a medium to high heat for a minute or two, tossing regularly, until the spices turn a couple of shades darker and begin to smell aromatic. Remove them from the pan immediately and grind, using a pestle and mortar or a spice grinder.

Melt the butter in a saucepan over a medium to high heat. When it foams, add the chopped onions, potatoes and carrots, and the freshly ground spices. Season with salt and pepper and toss until coated. Cover with a butter paper or a piece of parchment paper, and the saucepan lid. Turn the heat down to low and cook gently for about 10 minutes, stirring regularly, until the vegetables have just softened.

Remove the lid and paper and pour in the stock. Increase the heat and boil until the vegetables are completely tender. Pour into a liquidizer, add a squeeze of lemon juice and the cream or milk, and blend until smooth. Taste and adjust the seasoning.

Serve in warm bowls, with little blobs of crème fraîche or yoghurt on top and a scattering of coriander leaves, with a few toasted pitta wedges on the side.

notes   *If the potatoes that you're using are quite waxy, the soup might need a little extra stock to thin it out.*

If you have some leftover cooked carrots, they can be used in place of some or all of the carrots in the recipe here. Add with the stock and continue as opposite.

Pork and fennel meatball soup

This kind of soup reminds me of my favourite food as a child, and I still love it now. A meal in a bowl, with delicious but unchallenging flavours, it's a great one for feeding a crowd. If you want to make any of the elements of this soup in advance, the meatballs can be made and frozen, then thawed and cooked (see note overleaf) and the tomato soup can also be frozen.

For the soup

2 tablespoons extra virgin olive oil

1 onion, chopped

1 large celery stalk, chopped
  (see note)

1 carrot, peeled and chopped

2 large cloves of garlic, finely
  chopped

salt and freshly ground pepper

1 x 400g tin of plum tomatoes,
  chopped

2 teaspoons sugar

200ml cream (regular or double)

400–600ml chicken stock
  (see page 264)

150g spaghetti, broken into little bits

For the meatballs

3 tablespoons extra virgin olive oil

1 onion, finely chopped

1 large clove of garlic, crushed or
  finely grated

2 teaspoons fennel seeds, toasted
  and ground (see note)

450g minced pork

15g butter

To serve

a couple of handfuls of finely
  grated Parmesan

1 tablespoon chopped parsley

First, make the tomato soup. Place the olive oil in a saucepan over a medium heat and add the chopped onion, celery, carrot and garlic. Season with salt and pepper, cover with a butter wrapper or a piece of parchment paper, and the saucepan lid, then turn the heat down to low and cook for about 10–12 minutes, until the vegetables are tender, stirring every few minutes to prevent them sticking.

Add the tomatoes and sugar, season with more salt and pepper, and cook over a medium to high heat, uncovered, for about 10 minutes, until the tomatoes are melted through the sauce. Add the cream and boil for 3 minutes, then take off the heat.

Blend the sauce until completely smooth, then put back into the saucepan and add the stock to thin it out to the required consistency – you may want the soup a bit thicker, in which case just add 400–500ml of stock. Season to taste and set aside.

To make the meatballs, place 2 tablespoons of the olive oil in a saucepan and add the finely chopped onion and garlic. Season with salt and pepper, then cook over a low heat, covered with a butter wrapper or a piece of parchment paper and the saucepan lid, until the onions are tender, about 10 minutes. Take off the heat, tip the onions into a mixing bowl and allow to cool (see note overleaf).

While the onions are cooling, toast the fennel seeds in a dry frying pan over a medium to high heat. Crush them well, then add to the onions. Add the minced pork and mix

▶

well. Season with salt and pepper, then pick off ½ a teaspoonful of the mixture and cook it in a frying pan with a little olive oil and taste to check for seasoning. Add moresalt, pepper or ground fennel if necessary, then, when you're happy with the flavour, shape the meatballs. Make each one about 25g in weight (like a large walnut in its shell) – you should get about 20. Set them aside.

When you're ready to cook the meatballs, place a large frying pan on a medium heat and add the remaining olive oil and the butter (the butter helps the meatballs to brown really nicely). Once the butter has melted and foamed, add the meatballs and cook, tossing regularly, for about 8–10 minutes, until they are cooked through. Turn the heat down to low once they start to take on a golden hue.

While the meatballs are cooking, cook the spaghetti. Bring a saucepan of water to the boil, add a good pinch of salt, then add the broken pasta. Stir and allow to cook for 6–8 minutes, until al dente, then drain.

To serve, bring the tomato soup to steaming point and stir in the cooked pasta. Divide among bowls, then top with the meatballs and scatter finely grated Parmesan and chopped parsley over the top.

notes

When chopping the outer stalks of celery, it's a good idea to peel away the tough fibrous layer on the outside.

To toast the fennel seeds, place them in a dry frying pan over a medium to high heat and cook for about a minute, until fragrant and a couple of shades darker. Tip them out of the pan immediately and crush, using an electric spice grinder or a pestle and mortar. You can use ready-ground fennel but it might not taste as fresh and fragrant, in which case use slightly more, to taste.

If the meatballs are not being cooked immediately, it's essential that the onions cool completely before being added to the raw minced pork.

The meatballs can be made and frozen, then thawed and cooked, and the tomato soup can also be frozen. I like to tray-freeze the meatballs, which means I freeze them on a baking tray lined with parchment paper, then tip them into a box, cover with a lid, and store in the freezer until they're needed. That way, they won't stick together.

Ramen

Ramen is more than just a bowl of soup, for many it's almost a state of mind! People have devoted their whole lives, or a large proportion, to learning how to make the perfect ramen. A recipe that was originally imported from China, it is now one of Japan's most popular dishes, and ramen restaurants – or ramen-ya – are found on every corner throughout Japan.

I had the huge pleasure of working in Japan a few years ago and loved eating in ramen restaurants – in some of these you sit in a wooden booth for one person, with a hatch that goes up and down in front of you, where your bowl of ramen is placed by an invisible chef in the restaurant's galley kitchen behind. It's said that with no human interaction or other distractions you can savour the ramen wholeheartedly.

A bit like a car park, a seating chart with green or red buttons on the way into the dining room indicates available or taken seats. You order your ramen from a lit-up vending machine, clicking on the buttons to select everything you want in your bespoke bowl of deliciousness, from the broth and noodles to the many toppings, such as soft-boiled egg, rice, dried seaweed, mushrooms, beansprouts, spring onions and extra heat or garlic. Though you're eating alone, manners are still of the utmost importance, and noodle slurping is not only accepted, it's actually encouraged in order to cool the noodles while enjoying the hot broth.

While I don't claim to be a ramen master, or indeed an expert on Japanese food, I can assure you that this ramen is absolutely delicious, worth every minute of your time, and I hope it will leave you feeling like you've been transported to Japan in some little way.

The sesame garlic chilli sauce (see page 206) is a topping that I love to use on ramen. It keeps in the fridge for a couple of months and is divine on everything from roast meats to avocado on toast.

▶

Autumn – soup **broth** bread

750g piece of cooked pork shoulder
   or slow-roasted pork belly

extra virgin olive oil or vegetable oil

4 eggs

300g ramen noodles (or udon or
   soba noodles)

1.8 litres ramen broth (see page 278)

6 teaspoons shiro miso

8 teaspoons mirin (Japanese
   rice wine)

4 spring onions, sliced

sesame garlic chilli sauce
   (see page 206)

Shred the pork shoulder into long, thin pieces, or slice the slow-roasted pork belly into slices 7.5mm thick. Place a frying pan over a high heat, add a small drizzle of olive or vegetable oil, and cook the pork until golden brown and crisp on the outside. Set aside.

Bring a saucepan of water to the boil. Gently add 1 egg per person and boil for 6½ minutes, then drain and put them into a bowl of cold water. Leave until almost cool, then peel, discarding the shells. Set the eggs aside.

Fill the saucepan with water again and bring to the boil. Add the noodles and cook according to the instructions on the packet. Drain, then set aside.

Put the ramen broth into a saucepan. Add the shiro miso and mirin and bring to the boil, then pour into your deep ramen bowls. To each bowl add some of the noodles, and top with a soft-boiled egg, cut in half, the golden shredded or sliced pork, a generous tablespoon of sliced spring onions and a drizzle of sesame garlic chilli sauce.

Serve straight away with chopsticks and a spoon. Slurp and enjoy.

Curried butternut squash soup

Serves 4–6

Butternut squash is a perfect vehicle for spices and creamy coconut, and this silky-smooth soup has some great gutsy flavours. I adore the spicy pumpkin seed oil drizzled over the top for a contrast of textures. This is a super soup for making a large batch and freezing for a rainy day. Use other pumpkins or sweet potato in place of butternut if you wish.

 VG

 GF

For the soup

2 tablespoons coconut oil

1 large onion or 2 medium (200g in weight), chopped

1 butternut squash (600g when peeled and deseeded), peeled, deseeded and cut into 1cm cubes

1 large clove of garlic, chopped

salt and freshly ground pepper

1 x 400ml tin of coconut milk

1 tablespoon curry powder (see note)

450ml vegetable or chicken stock (see pages 277, 264)

For the garnish

1 tablespoon coconut oil

2 tablespoons pumpkin seeds

a pinch of curry powder

a pinch of sea salt flakes

Put the coconut oil into a saucepan over a medium heat. Add the chopped onions, butternut squash and garlic. Season with salt and pepper and stir to mix. Turn the heat down to low, cover the vegetables with a piece of parchment paper and the saucepan lid, and allow to cook slowly for 10 minutes, stirring from time to time, until they are tender.

Meanwhile, pour the coconut milk into a bowl and whisk to remove any lumps.

Remove the paper cover and lid from the pan and stir in the curry powder. Turn the heat up to high and cook, stirring, for a minute, until the curry powder is wonderfully fragrant. Now add the coconut milk and the stock and bring to a rolling boil, then blend the soup until gorgeously smooth.

To make the toasted pumpkin seeds, place a frying pan over a high heat and add the coconut oil. Allow to melt and heat up, then add the pumpkin seeds and curry powder. Toss over the heat for 1–2 minutes, until the seeds have toasted and darkened slightly, then place on a plate lined with kitchen paper and sprinkle with the sea salt flakes.

Serve the soup steaming hot, with the toasted pumpkin seeds scattered over the top.

notes
If your curry powder has been hanging around your kitchen for a year or more, it has probably gone a bit stale and could be almost tasteless. Buy a new batch for the best fresh spicy flavour – the difference will really enhance your soup.

If you're not wanting this soup to be vegan, and you have a leftover butter wrapper in your fridge (I always hang on to mine for this reason), you can place it, butter side down, over the vegetables while they're cooking instead of using parchment paper.

Potato, parsley and thyme soup with chorizo

Serves 4–6

A potato soup is so versatile and works superbly with spices, fresh herbs, pestos and drizzles. I prefer to use floury potatoes, rather than waxy, for the lightest, silkiest consistency. If reheating this soup, avoid prolonged simmering, to retain its silky texture. This soup is also delicious unblended and served chunky.

(GF)

25g butter
350g peeled and chopped potatoes
150g peeled and chopped onions
sea salt and freshly ground pepper
750ml chicken or vegetable stock
  (see page 264, 277)

1 tablespoon chopped parsley
1 teaspoon chopped thyme
250ml milk, or half milk and
  half cream
75g chorizo
1 tablespoon extra virgin olive oil

Melt the butter in a saucepan over a medium heat until it foams. Add the chopped potatoes and onions, season with salt and pepper, then stir well and cover with a butter wrapper or a piece of parchment paper. Add the pan lid and sweat over a gentle heat for 10 minutes, stirring occasionally to prevent the potatoes sticking.

Add the stock, bring to the boil, and cook until the vegetables are all tender. Add the chopped herbs and milk (or milk and cream), liquidize the soup and season to taste.

While the vegetables are cooking, peel the chorizo and cut into small dice. Pour the olive oil into a cool frying pan. Add the chorizo, then place the pan on a very low heat and gently cook for a few minutes, turning the chorizo every so often. Done over a very low heat like this, you'll end up with beautifully cooked chorizo with the rich amber-coloured oils rendered out. You want both the oils and the chorizo itself for drizzling over the soup when serving. Take off when it is crisp, reserving the rendered oil.

Reheat the soup if necessary, then pour into warm bowls and top with a few pieces of cooked chorizo, with a drizzle of the oil from the pan over the top.

note   *You can use leftover mash in place of some or all of the raw potato, but instead of adding at the start, stir it in when the milk goes in and continue as above. Other leftover vegetables, such as cooked carrots, broccoli, parsnips or even spinach, can be added with the milk, keeping in mind that you may need extra stock and milk to thin it out at the end.*

Fish ball laksa

A spicy coconut-based noodle soup from South East Asia, there are probably millions of different versions of laksa. Rich and spicy, laksa can include meat, seafood or tofu, or all three, with the noodles, which can be.thin rice noodles (vermicelli noodles), thick wheat noodles, or even a combination of the two. I have travelled quite a bit around South East Asia and always try to seek out a local laksa to enjoy. One of my favourites in Malaysia is a fish ball laksa, which inspired this recipe here. I hope you enjoy it as much as I do. I guarantee that you won't regret spending your time making this divine bowl of deliciousness.

For the fish balls

175g white fish, such as round or flat fish (whatever is freshest), filleted, skinned and cut into chunks (weight when filleted and skinned)

1 tablespoon soy sauce

2½ teaspoons cornflour

For the laksa paste

1–2 red chillies (depending on how hot you love your laksa!)

3 shallots (50g when peeled)

2 teaspoons peeled and chopped fresh galangal or ginger (10g in weight)

2 stalks of lemongrass

1½ teaspoons shrimp paste

1 teaspoon ground turmeric

2 tablespoons water

For the broth

3 tablespoons olive or sunflower oil

1 x 400ml tin of coconut milk

1 litre fish stock (see page 272)

300g noodles, about 75g per person (see note)

3 tablespoons fish sauce (nam pla)

juice of ½–1 lime

225g firm tofu, cut into 2cm cubes

75g beansprouts

4 eggs, boiled for 6–7 minutes, then peeled and halved

a small handful of coriander leaves

crispy fried shallots (see page 202)

To make the fish balls, put the chopped fish into a food processor or blender with the soy sauce and the cornflour, and blend until you have a sticky paste.

Using clean and slightly damp hands, roll the mixture into 20 balls, each one weighing 9 or 10g each. Place on a plate or a tray and chill for at least 30 minutes, until you're ready to cook them.

Put all the laksa paste ingredients into a food processor or blender and blend until the mixture forms a paste.

Pour 1 tablespoon of the oil into a saucepan over a medium heat and add the paste. Stir and fry until fragrant, about 4–5 minutes. Now add the coconut milk and stock and bring the mixture to the boil, turning the heat up to high.

Meanwhile, cook the noodles according to the instructions on the packet. Drain, leaving a few tablespoons of the noodle liquid in with the noodles (to stop them sticking) and set aside.

Add the fish balls to the boiling coconut broth and cook over a medium to high heat for 6–7 minutes, until they are cooked. You can cut one in half to check; it should be opaque all the way through. Add the fish sauce to season, according to your taste – you might want just 2 or 3 tablespoons but you might want more. Add lime juice to taste.

Meanwhile, heat the remaining 2 tablespoons of olive or sunflower oil in a frying pan over a high heat. Add the tofu and fry on all sides until golden and crispy, approximately 5 minutes. Drain on kitchen paper and set aside, somewhere warm preferably.

Put the noodles into bowls and divide out the beansprouts, placing them on top of the noodles. Pour the hot broth over the top, then divide the fish balls and the golden fried tofu among the bowls. Top with 2 halves of softly-boiled egg per bowl, sprinkle with coriander leaves and crispy fried shallots, and serve.

 notes *I normally reckon on 75g of noodles per person for a big bowl of laksa, and I generally just use rice noodles. In Malaysia they often use 50g of Hokkien noodles for every 25g of rice noodles (usually rice vermicelli, the thin noodles), but sometimes they just use rice vermicelli and no Hokkien noodles – so use what you like!*

Ready-made fish balls often have lots of preservatives and additives in them, and they're so easy to make from scratch. They can also be frozen.

You can use prawns or shrimps instead of the fish balls if you wish. Use 175g of raw prawns or shrimps, halved lengthwise if big, and cook them in the broth like the fish balls, until opaque all the way through, approximately 3–4 minutes.

A laksa like this will often include tofu puffs, which you can buy ready-made, but I prefer to shallow-fry firm tofu for this.

Chunky chickpea and chorizo broth

Serves 4–6

Bringing together two of my favourite ingredients, this is such a comforting bowl of soup. The chickpeas give great texture, the chorizo delivers its characteristic punchy flavour, which I adore, and the fresh coriander adds a verdant hit of goodness. You can use fresh parsley instead of the coriander if you prefer.

(GF)

1 tablespoon extra virgin olive oil

150g chorizo, diced

1 onion, finely chopped

2 celery stalks, finely chopped

2 cloves of garlic, crushed or grated

salt and freshly ground pepper

1 x 400g tin of chickpeas, or 120g dried chickpeas, soaked overnight

in plenty of cold water and cooked (see note)

2 x 400g tins of plum tomatoes, chopped, or 8 fresh ripe tomatoes, peeled (see note, page 76) and chopped

750ml chicken stock (see page 264)

2 tablespoons chopped fresh coriander leaves

Place the olive oil in a large saucepan on a low heat and immediately add the diced chorizo. Cook for a few minutes until the chorizo releases its oils (if the heat is too high, the chorizo will brown before it releases its oils), then add the chopped onion, celery and garlic. Season with salt and pepper and cook on a gentle heat, with a lid, until the onion is completely cooked, about 10 minutes, stirring occasionally. Now remove the lid, turn the heat up high and cook for a minute to slightly brown the onion.

Add the chickpeas (including all the liquid from the tins – or if cooking from dried, add 400ml of the cooking liquid), the tomatoes with all their liquid, and the stock, season with salt and pepper and bring to the boil.

Simmer for about 20 minutes, until the tomatoes have melted into the broth, and the chickpeas have absorbed all the flavours. Taste for seasoning, and add more salt and pepper if necessary – you might also need a large pinch of sugar. Serve in deep, warm bowls, sprinkled with the chopped coriander.

note *To cook dried chickpeas: Soak in cold water overnight, then drain, cover with fresh water and cook until tender – this can take 40–60 minutes, depending on their age. Drain, reserving the cooking liquid.*

Cockle and mussel soup
with chorizo and saffron

Serves 6

Cockles and mussels are both nutritious and sustainable, and when combined with chorizo and saffron you get a fabulously bold-flavoured soup that's inspired by some of my favourite Spanish tapas. Don't forget to check over each and every cockle and mussel to make sure that they are tightly shut or, if not, that they close when tapped on the worktop, otherwise they could be dead and have gone bad. Discard any that aren't alive.

(GF)

4 tablespoons extra virgin olive oil

1 small onion, sliced

1.5kg mixture of cockles and mussels, scrubbed and de-bearded (see note)

125ml white wine

150g chorizo, finely diced

2 medium carrots, finely diced

2 medium leeks, white and pale green parts only, finely chopped

2 cloves of garlic, crushed or finely grated

salt and freshly ground pepper

1 x 400g tin of plum tomatoes, chopped

a large pinch of sugar

½ teaspoon saffron threads

850ml fish stock (see page 272)

2 tablespoons chopped parsley

a squeeze of lemon juice (approximately 1 tablespoon)

Place a large saucepan on a medium heat, add 2 tablespoons of the olive oil and the sliced onion and stir to mix. Turn the heat down to low and cook the onion slowly for 8 10 minutes, until softened but not coloured.

While the onion is cooking, scrub the mussels and cockles in a sink or bowl of cold water. Pull away the beard from each mussel (the fibrous tuft that attaches the straight side of the mussel to the rock or rope that it grows on) and scrub off any barnacles. Check each cockle and mussel. If any of them are open and do not close when tapped against the work surface, discard them, as they could be dead and not fresh. Set aside all the good tightly closed cockles and mussels.

Add the white wine to the onions, then increase the heat to high and bring to the boil. Add the cockles and mussels, cover with the saucepan lid, and cook until the shells open, about 4 minutes. Discard any that don't open. Tip the cockles and mussels into a colander or large sieve sitting over a bowl to collect the precious

▶

cooking liquid. Set the liquid aside and remove the cockles and mussels from their shells, discarding the shells (keep a few aside for garnishing the soup if you wish) and the sliced onions.

Add the remaining 2 tablespoons of olive oil to the saucepan and place on a medium heat. Add the diced chorizo, carrots, leeks and garlic, and season with salt and pepper. Turn the heat down to low and cook, covered with the saucepan lid, stirring occasionally, for 8–10 minutes, until the vegetables have softened. Turn up the heat to medium and add the tinned tomatoes, a large pinch of sugar, the saffron, the fish stock and the reserved cockle and mussel cooking liquid, and bring to the boil. Simmer the soup for about 20–30 minutes, until the tomatoes have completely softened.

Now add the cooked cockles and mussels and simmer for 1 minute, just so the cockles and mussels are heated through (don't be tempted to cook for longer, as overcooking renders them tough and chewy). Add most of the chopped parsley and some lemon juice to taste, and season with more salt and pepper if you wish. Ladle the soup into deep, warm bowls, arranging a few opened shells on top with cockles and mussels in them, and lastly, scatter over the rest of the parsley.

 note   *Sometimes I make this soup with either just cockles or just mussels, both of which are delicious variations.*

Lentil soup with lemon and parsley

Serves 4–6

Supremely simple, this soup really is more than the sum of its parts. There are many versions of this in the Middle East, where it's sometimes called *shorbat ads*, literally meaning 'soup of lentils'. The success of this comforting soup relies on the balance of the lemon juice, salt and spices.

 VG

 GF

2 tablespoons extra virgin olive oil
1 onion, finely chopped
2 cloves of garlic, finely chopped
salt and freshly ground pepper
1 teaspoon ground turmeric
2 teaspoons ground cumin (see note)

150g yellow or orange lentils
1.2 litres vegetable or chicken stock (see pages 277, 264)
2 tablespoons chopped parsley
juice of ½–1 lemon

Place the olive oil in a saucepan over a medium heat. Add the finely chopped onions and garlic, and season with salt and pepper. Turn the heat down to low and cover the onions with a piece of parchment paper, and the saucepan lid. Cook, stirring from time to time, for 10 minutes, until the onions are tender.

Add the turmeric and cumin and stir, with the heat turned up to medium-high, for 2 minutes, until the spices are fragrant, then add the lentils. Stir over the heat until they're all coated with the onions, then add the stock. Bring to the boil, then turn the heat down and cook with the lid on for about 20 minutes, until the lentils are completely cooked and have almost disintegrated into a mush.

Add the parsley, season with lemon juice and more salt and pepper if necessary, then serve in warm bowls.

note   *I always toast and grind my own cumin rather than buying it ready ground, as the flavour is so much better. Just place the cumin seeds in a dry frying pan over a medium to high heat and cook, tossing regularly, for a couple of minutes, until the seeds are a few shades darker and fragrant. Then tip out of the pan and crush in a spice grinder or using a pestle and mortar.*

Roasted parsnip and cauliflower soup with smoked paprika

Serves 6

I love the combination of nutty cumin and smoky paprika used in Middle Eastern cuisine, which also works so well in this smooth and velvety soup. Topped with the roasted vegetables and the smoked paprika oil, this soup is supremely simple, completely delicious, and just perfect on a cold day.

3 tablespoons extra virgin olive oil

2 medium parsnips (450g in weight)

1 small head of cauliflower

2 large red onions, peeled and cut into chunks

2 teaspoons smoked paprika

2½ teaspoons ground cumin

salt and freshly ground pepper

1.25 litres vegetable or chicken stock (see pages 277, 264)

For the smoked paprika oil

1 teaspoon smoked paprika

2 tablespoons extra virgin olive oil

Preheat the oven to 220°C/200°C fan/gas 7. Place the olive oil in a large mixing bowl. Cut the parsnips into quarters, remove and discard the tough cores, then cut them into 1cm chunks. Add these to the olive oil in the bowl. Now remove the tough outer green leaves from the cauliflower and cut off the base of the stem. Cut the cauliflower into florets and add these to the parsnips, along with the red onion chunks. Scatter over the smoked paprika, cumin and some salt and pepper and toss well together.

Lay the vegetables and all the oil in a single layer on a large roasting or baking tray and roast for 30 minutes, or until the vegetables are golden around the edges, and tender.

Now remove 3 tablespoons of the vegetables (these will be scattered over the soup when serving, so save some nice-looking florets and parsnip and onion chunks) and blend the remaining vegetables with the stock until smooth, adding more stock if it is a bit thick. Pour into a saucepan, heat through and season to taste.

Mix the smoked paprika with the olive oil and set aside.

Reheat the soup if necessary, then serve in bowls, with a few pieces of roast vegetables arranged on top and a drizzle of smoked paprika oil.

note   *I use sweet smoked paprika for this soup, but you can also use hot smoked paprika.*

Prawn gumbo with spicy sausage and bourbon

Serves 4

This great stew-like soup that my husband Zac made on our return from a fabulous trip to New Orleans a couple of years ago, while not an authentic Southern recipe, is gumbo-inspired and has a definite feel of Louisiana about it. It's quite rich, so it works well in small portions, and feel free to use a different whiskey if you wish.

25g butter

3–4 cloves of garlic, crushed or finely grated

300g raw prawns or shrimps, peeled and cut in half lengthwise if large

1 teaspoon Tabasco

50g spicy sausage such as kabanosi, chorizo or pepperoni, thinly sliced

salt and freshly ground pepper

3 tablespoons Bourbon whiskey

1 x 400g tin of plum tomatoes, chopped

400ml chicken stock (see page 264)

125ml cream (regular or double)

15g finely grated hard cheese, such as Parmesan

2 teaspoons chopped thyme

To serve

15g grated hard cheese, such as Parmesan

1 lime, cut into wedges

Melt the butter in a saucepan over a medium heat. Add the garlic, the prawns or shrimps, the Tabasco and the sliced spicy sausage. Season with salt and pepper, then cook, gently stirring occasionally, for about 4 minutes, until the prawns or shrimps turn opaque.

Add the whiskey and allow to bubble for 1 minute, then pour in the chopped tomatoes with all their juices, and the stock. Cook the soup gently, covered with a lid, for about 10 minutes, then add the cream and allow to bubble for about 5 minutes.

Finally, add the grated cheese and the chopped thyme and season to taste. Serve the gumbo in warmed bowls, with grated hard cheese to scatter over the top and wedges of lime to squeeze.

Kale and sausage chunky broth with fennel and lemon

Serves 4–6

Homely and comforting, this soup uses crushed fennel seeds and lemon zest, which complement the pork sausages so well, giving the soup a lovely freshness that's redolent of the Italian flavours I adore. Use chard or spinach in place of the kale if you like.

(GF)

3 tablespoons extra virgin olive oil

1 large onion, thinly sliced

salt, freshly ground pepper and a good pinch of sugar

2 large cloves of garlic, peeled and thinly sliced

1½ teaspoons fennel seeds, crushed

4 strips of lemon peel

6 sausages, cut into 1cm slices

1 x 400g tin of plum tomatoes, chopped

750ml chicken, duck or goose stock (see pages 264, 268, 269)

75g kale (weight after it has been de-stalked), thinly shredded

Place 2 tablespoons of the olive oil in a saucepan over a medium heat and add the sliced onions. Season with salt and pepper, then turn the heat down slightly and cook the onions, uncovered, for about 6–8 minutes, until softened and slightly golden around the edges. Add the sliced garlic, the fennel seeds and the lemon peel strips and cook for 2–3 minutes more, until the garlic, fennel and lemon are aromatic.

Now scrape all the ingredients from the saucepan on to a plate, set aside and place the pan back on the heat, turning it up to medium-high. Add the remaining tablespoon of olive oil to the pan and, when it's hot, add the sausage slices. Cook them on all sides, until golden, then tip the onions, garlic, fennel and lemon peel back into the pan with all their juices. Add the chopped tomatoes and the stock, and season with more salt and pepper and a good pinch of sugar to help balance the acidity from the tomatoes.

Bring the mixture to the boil, then turn the heat down and simmer for 15 minutes, until the tomatoes have melted completely. Correct the seasoning, then turn the heat up high, add the shredded kale and cook until the kale is tender, about 4 minutes.

Serve in deep bowls, with crusty bread.

note   *If making this with fresh tomatoes, use 400g of peeled, chopped tomatoes (see page 76).*

Congee

In China there are as many different names for the soupy rice porridge congee as there are different versions of it. A breakfast dish eaten across China, made with rice and water and sometimes other starchy ingredients too, such as sweet potato, pumpkin, mung or adzuki beans, or millet, congee is the ultimate in comfort food, though because of its starchy porridgy texture, it can be divisive; I love it. It's very easy to digest, so it's good to eat if you're feeling under the weather.

In the north of China it's often plain congee that's eaten, whereas in the southern regions, and particularly in Hong Kong, congee is served with various toppings, including meat, tofu and vegetables.

This is my version of a really simple Cantonese congee, called *jook*, with soft-boiled egg, crispy shallots and spring onions. Sometimes a little chilli oil is added, and if you happen to have any sesame garlic chilli sauce (see page 206), a small drizzle of this works well too. Sometimes minced pork, chicken or fish is added just before the end of cooking and simmered until the protein is cooked, or meat, fish, or tofu can be sliced and cooked separately (sometimes with a soy, ginger and garlic marinade) before being served on top of the congee. If fresh or dried fish is used in the congee, a drizzle of fish sauce is used in place of the soy.

The rice that you use for congee needs to be starchy, so something like a long-grain jasmine rice or medium-grain Japanese japonica rice (also called sushi rice) works well to give the creamy and silky texture that you want.

The longer that congee sits after being cooked, the thicker it gets, as it will continue to absorb the liquid, so if you're making it in advance and reheating it, just add a little more stock or water. I love to use chicken stock for added flavour and nutrition.

The bao buns (see page 257) with a filling of sticky pork with sesame (see page 205), unsurprisingly, are great with a bowl of congee.

200g rice

2.5 litres chicken stock
(see page 264)

1cm piece of fresh ginger,
cut into 4 slices

a pinch of salt

To serve

1 egg per person

4 tablespoons crispy fried shallots
(see page 202)

3 spring onions, sliced very thinly
at an angle

a few coriander leaves

Chinese light soy sauce

First, rinse the rice very briefly, then drain it and place it in a saucepan with the chicken stock, ginger slices and a pinch of salt. Put the saucepan on a medium heat and bring to the boil, then turn the heat down to low, stirring to prevent the rice sticking to the base of the pot. Cover with a lid, slightly at an angle to let the steam escape, and cook the congee for 1½–2 hours, stirring every 10 minutes or so, until the rice is completely tender and broken down, giving you a thin porridge consistency.

While the rice is cooking, place the eggs in a saucepan over a medium heat and cover with boiling water. Bring the water back to the boil and cook the eggs for 5–7 minutes, depending on their size, then drain. Crack the shells gently, then peel.

Pour the congee into bowls, and top with the crispy fried shallots, sliced spring onion, a few coriander leaves and a drizzle of soy sauce. Cut the soft-boiled eggs in half and place one on top of each bowl, then serve.

 note *I find that jasmine rice absorbs less liquid than japonica rice, so if using jasmine rice, you'll probably just need 1.9 litres of stock.*

WINTER

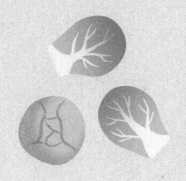

Cauliflower, cashew and coriander soup

Serves 6

This smooth and creamy golden bowl of goodness gets its silky texture from cashew nuts and its soothing anti-inflammatory benefits from the yellow turmeric. Serve on its own, or with toasted cashews scattered over the top.

1 cauliflower head

3 tablespoons extra virgin olive oil

1 large onion (200g), chopped

4 large cloves of garlic, chopped

100g cashews

1 tablespoon ground turmeric

½ teaspoon freshly ground
black pepper

a few good pinches of salt

1.1 litres vegetable or chicken stock
(see pages 277, 264)

2 tablespoons lemon juice

4 tablespoons chopped coriander
(leaves and the fine stalks)

For the toasted cashews

20g cashews

First, prepare the cauliflower. Remove and discard the outer green leaves, reserving any smaller ones close to the cauliflower, and cut off and discard the base of the stem. Cut the cauliflower into slices, then chop it all: florets, stalks and any remaining leaves.

Place the olive oil in a saucepan over a medium heat and add the cauliflower, the chopped onion and garlic, the cashews and the turmeric. Season with the pepper and a few good pinches of salt (this soup needs careful seasoning, otherwise it can be bland).

Cover the vegetables with the saucepan lid, then turn the heat down to low and cook, stirring from time to time, for about 15–20 minutes, until the vegetables are tender.

While the vegetables are cooking, toast the cashews. Place them in a dry frying pan over a medium heat and toss them regularly for about 4 minutes, until golden. Roughly chop and set aside.

Add the stock to the vegetables and bring to the boil, then blend the soup well. Add the lemon juice, chopped coriander and more salt and pepper if necessary. The soup should be smooth, like velvet.

Serve the soup straight away or reheat, and scatter the toasted cashews over the top.

Jerusalem artichoke soup with chorizo, avocado and almond salsa

Serves 8–10

We make this deliciously nutritious soup at the cookery school once the Jerusalem artichokes come into season in the autumn. Depending on the variety, they can be a bit knobbly and are a slight fiddle to peel, but do persevere as they taste so good and have been applauded for their sky-high nutritional content.

This smooth blended soup is lovely just on its own or with croutons, but if you want to bring in some more great textures and flavours, I recommend the avocado and roast hazelnut salsa below, or the chorizo crumbs (see page 191).

50g butter

560g onions, peeled and chopped

1kg Jerusalem artichokes, scrubbed, peeled and chopped

salt and freshly ground pepper

1.1 litres chicken or vegetable stock (see page 264, 277)

300ml milk

300ml cream (regular or double) (or you can use 600ml milk and no cream)

For the salsa

75g chorizo

1 tablespoon extra virgin olive oil

2 tablespoons almonds, preferably with their skins on, sliced lengthways, slightly coarsely

1 ripe avocado, peeled, stoned and diced into neat scant 1cm dice

1 tablespoon chopped parsley

Melt the butter in a large saucepan over a medium heat, add the onions and the artichokes. Season with salt and freshly ground pepper, cover with a butter wrapper or a piece of parchment paper and the saucepan lid and cook gently, over a low heat, for 10 minutes, stirring every few minutes. After 10 minutes, add the stock and cook over a high heat until the vegetables are tender. Add in the milk and blend well, taste for seasoning and add in the cream.

While the soup is cooking, make the salsa. Peel the chorizo and cut into small dice, about 5mm. Place in a frying pan (do not preheat the pan), drizzle over the olive oil and leave over a low heat to cook very slowly for about 5 minutes. You want to allow the rich amber oils to render out of the chorizo before the chorizo has a chance to brown. Take the chorizo out of the pan and set it aside in a bowl, leaving all the oil in the pan.

▶

Add the chopped almonds to the chorizo oil in the pan and cook them over a medium heat for a few minutes, until golden and toasted, tossing them regularly to ensure even cooking. Tip the almonds and all the oil into the bowl of chorizo and allow to cool.

Add the avocado and parsley and season to taste. If the salsa is a little thick, add another drizzle of olive oil. You can serve the salsa straight away, or cover and leave in your fridge for up to 1 hour.

Serve the soup in warm bowls, with blobs of chorizo, avocado and almond salsa over the top.

Simple celery and nutmeg soup

The humble celery, which can often be overlooked in favour of more exciting vegetables, is at the backbone of so many classic recipes, not least in soups, broths and stocks. As well as helping to reduce inflammation and aid digestion, celery is thought to be rich in vitamins and minerals, and a great source of antioxidants; what's not to love?

In this recipe there's lots of garlic and a little nutmeg too to notch up the flavour, giving you a delicious and nutritious bowl of soup that also happens to freeze really well. Use extra virgin olive oil in place of the butter for a dairy-free version.

25g butter

1½ large onions (300g), chopped

6 large celery stalks (375g), chopped

5 cloves of garlic, chopped

salt and freshly ground pepper

750ml vegetable or chicken stock (see pages 277, 264)

½ teaspoon grated nutmeg

Put the butter into a saucepan over a medium heat and melt until foaming. Add the onion, celery and garlic and season with salt and pepper. Cover with a butter wrapper or a piece of parchment paper and the saucepan lid. Turn the heat down to low and cook really gently, stirring from time to time, for 10 minutes, until the celery is tender.

Add the stock and the nutmeg and turn the heat up to high. Bring the mixture up to the boil and cook for 2 minutes, then blend until smooth.

Season to taste, adding a little more nutmeg if necessary. Serve steaming hot, in mugs or bowls.

Lamb and pearl barley broth

Serves 6–8

This is a seriously substantial bowl of soup. Nurturing, restorative and oh, so comforting, this is the kind of soup I crave if I'm feeling under the weather with a cold. It's a great way to use up leftover cooked lamb, but cooked chicken or pork also work well in this soup.

25g butter

2 tablespoons extra virgin olive oil

2 medium onions, finely chopped

2 celery stalks, finely chopped

2 cloves of garlic, crushed or finely grated

1 bay leaf

1 sprig of rosemary

salt and freshly ground pepper

200g leftover cooked lamb, sliced or shredded

1 medium parsnip, peeled and finely chopped

2 medium carrots, peeled and finely chopped

100g pearl barley (or pearled spelt)

1.25 litres chicken stock (see page 264)

2 tablespoons chopped parsley

Place the butter and olive oil in a large saucepan over a medium heat. Once the butter is melted and foaming, add the onions, celery, garlic, bay leaf and rosemary sprig. Season with salt and pepper, then turn the heat to low, cover and cook gently for 10 minutes, or until the onions are softened.

Add the lamb, the chopped parsnip and carrot, the pearl barley and the stock. Turn the heat up and simmer, covered, for about 25–30 minutes, until the vegetables and barley are deliciously tender.

Remove the bay and rosemary. Stir in the chopped parsley, season again to taste, then serve.

Brussels sprout soup with candied bacon and roasted hazelnuts

Serves 6

A most Christmassy soup, with the candied bacon and roasted hazelnuts bringing a festive flavour and delicious crunch to the sprouts. To get ahead, make the soup in advance and freeze it. The candied bacon can be made hours in advance of serving, and the hazelnuts can even be roasted a couple of days ahead.

For the soup
50g butter
175g peeled and diced potatoes
175g peeled and diced onions
salt and freshly ground pepper
400g Brussels sprouts
1.1 litres chicken stock (see page 264)
250ml cream or milk, or a mixture

For the roasted hazelnuts
50g hazelnuts

For the candied bacon
25g soft light brown sugar, such as light Muscovado sugar
6 slices of streaky bacon (smoked if you wish)

First, make the soup. Melt the butter in a large saucepan over a medium heat. When it foams, add the potatoes and onions, season with salt and pepper, and stir to mix. Cover with a butter wrapper or a piece of parchment paper, then turn the heat down to low, cover with the saucepan lid and cook on a gentle heat for 10 minutes, stirring every few minutes to prevent the vegetables sticking and burning.

While the potatoes and onions are cooking, prepare the sprouts. Trim the base, remove and discard the outer two or three leaves, and slice the sprouts thinly. Set aside.

When the potatoes and onions have been cooking for 10 minutes, add the chicken stock and boil for 2–3 minutes, until the potatoes are tender.

Add the sliced sprouts to the pan and cook over a high heat, with the lid off, until tender, approximately 2–3 minutes. Do not overcook, or the sprouts will lose their fresh colour and flavour. Add the cream or milk and blend until smooth. If you want the soup to be a bit thinner, add a little more stock. Taste for seasoning.

To prepare the hazelnuts and the bacon, preheat the oven to 200°C/180°C fan/gas 6.

Place the hazelnuts on a baking tray and roast in the preheated oven for 6–8 minutes, checking regularly, as they can burn quickly. To test them, take the tray out of the oven

▸

and carefully rub the skins off a few of them – the nuts should be golden underneath. When ready, tip them out of the tray and on to a clean tea towel, and rub to remove the skins. Discard the skins and chop the nuts coarsely. Set aside until you're ready to use them.

To make the candied bacon, line a baking tray with a sheet of parchment paper. Place the brown sugar in a bowl and dip both sides of the streaky bacon in it so that they are completely coated. Use a little more sugar if you need to. Cook for 5–6 minutes in the preheated oven, until the bacon is caramelized on both sides. Remove from the oven and leave until cool and crisp. Once crisp, break the bacon, or snip with scissors, into pieces about 1cm in size.

Reheat the soup gently until steaming, then pour into bowls and scatter over the roasted hazelnuts and candied bacon. Serve immediately.

notes   *For a vegetarian version, you can use vegetable stock instead of chicken, and omit the candied bacon.*

If this soup is to be reheated, just bring it to steaming point and serve. Prolonged boiling spoils the colour and flavour of green soups and also this soup's smooth, silky texture.

Oxtail soup
with gremolata

Serves 10–12

Oxtail is a great but often under-used cut of beef. There isn't a huge amount of meat on an oxtail, but what you do get is deliciously rich and flavoursome. The intensely refreshing gremolata cuts through and complements the richness perfectly. A wonderful bowl of soup for a blustery day.

2–3 tablespoons olive oil

1.5kg oxtail, cut into pieces (see note), and trimmed of excess fat

salt and freshly ground pepper

1 large onion, peeled and chopped

2 carrots, peeled and chopped

3 celery stalks, trimmed and sliced

2 large cloves of garlic

250ml red wine

1 bay leaf

1 sprig of thyme

1 tablespoon tomato purée

1 tablespoon Worcestershire sauce

2 litres beef stock (see page 270)

For the gremolata

finely grated zest of 1 lemon

1 clove of garlic, crushed or finely grated

2 tablespoons finely chopped parsley

Place a large saucepan or casserole pot on a high heat and allow to get hot. Drizzle in 1–2 tablespoons of the olive oil and fry the oxtail pieces in batches, adding a little more olive oil if necessary, for 4–5 minutes in total, or until they are well browned all over, seasoning them with salt and pepper as they cook. Remove from the pan and set aside.

Add another tablespoon of olive oil to the pot and tip in the chopped onion, carrots, celery and garlic, season with salt and pepper, then cover with a butter wrapper or a sheet of parchment paper and a tight-fitting lid and cook on a very gentle heat for 8–10 minutes, stirring occasionally, until the vegetables are just tender.

Return the oxtail pieces to the pot and add the red wine, bay leaf, thyme, tomato purée and Worcestershire sauce. Season with salt and pepper, then pour in the stock and bring slowly to the boil, skimming off any frothy impurities that rise to the surface. Reduce the heat to very low, cover with the lid and gently simmer for about 3 hours, or until the meat is almost falling off the bone. Continue to occasionally skim off any impurities as well as any rendered fat.

Remove from the heat and strain through a colander over a large bowl to catch the

▸

liquid. Tip the meat and vegetables into a large, shallow bowl and leave to cool a little. Add a few ice cubes to the liquid and wait for the fat to rise to the top, then remove and discard it. Once the meat and vegetables are cool enough to handle, discard the bay leaf and thyme sprig and remove the meat from the oxtail bones.

Pour the liquid into a blender with the reserved vegetables and two-thirds of the meat (you may have to do this in batches) and blitz to a smooth soup, then return it to the pan. Add the remaining shards of meat and bring slowly to the boil.

Mix together the ingredients for the gremolata, then check the seasoning and serve the soup in warm bowls, with the gremolata scattered over the top.

 notes *To cut the oxtail into pieces, using a sharp knife, slice between the bones where they are connected to each other with tissue similar to ligament – it's easier if you feel with your fingers first where the joints are. Where the oxtail is thick and wide, at the top end, cut at every joint, but where the oxtail is thin and skinny, cut at every second or third joint.*

For an alcohol-free version of this soup, just omit the red wine and use extra stock, though do bear in mind that a lot of alcohol evaporates in cooking anyway.

The gremolata is wonderful scattered over rich beef soups, such as the oxtail soup above, or the chunky beef and stout soup (see page 168), or hearty winter vegetable soups, such as the roasted parsnip and cauliflower soup (see page 133).

Sausage, bean and spinach broth

Serves 6–8

A lovely recipe that I return to time and time again when I am yearning for something soothing and reassuring. The small splash of sherry vinegar or red wine vinegar added at the end creates the perfect balance with all the other flavours. You could use an equivalent amount of kale, chard, wild garlic or even nettles instead of the spinach if you'd like a variation.

3 tablespoons extra virgin olive oil

1 medium onion, finely chopped

1 medium carrot, finely chopped

1 celery stalk, finely chopped

2 large garlic cloves, finely chopped

sea salt and freshly ground pepper

2 x 400g tins of white beans
 (such as haricot beans), drained

1 litre chicken or vegetable stock
 (see pages 264, 277)

3 sprigs of thyme

1 bay leaf

6 medium sausages

200g spinach (weight after removing
 any large stalks), sliced

1 tablespoon sherry vinegar or red
 wine vinegar

1 tablespoon chopped parsley

Place a large saucepan on a medium heat, add 2 tablespoons of the olive oil and when warm add the onions, carrots, celery and garlic. Season with salt and pepper, then turn the heat down and cook, covered with the saucepan lid, stirring occasionally, for 10–12 minutes, until tender.

Add the beans, stock, thyme and bay leaf and bring to the boil, then reduce the heat and cook, covered, on a low simmer for about 10 minutes.

Meanwhile, put 1 tablespoon of olive oil into a frying pan and place on a medium heat. Add the sausages and cook, tossing regularly, for a few minutes on each side, until well browned all over and cooked through. Remove the sausages from the pan and cut into pieces roughly 1cm across.

Add the sliced spinach to the soup, then bring back to the boil over a high heat and simmer for 2–3 minutes, until the spinach is tender. Remove and discard the thyme and bay leaf. Add the sausages to the soup, then stir in the sherry vinegar or red wine vinegar, whichever you're using, and taste for seasoning. Serve steaming hot in bowls, with a sprinkling of chopped parsley.

Chinese-style duck broth with noodles

Serves 4

This delicious soup can be made with either duck or chicken stock. The latter gives a slightly different outcome, lighter in flavour but still delicious, whereas duck stock made with roasted bones gives a deep richness that works so well with these Chinese flavours.

100g thin rice noodles

600ml Asian duck or chicken stock (see pages 269, 264)

2 x 5mm slices of fresh ginger, slightly bashed

2 cloves of garlic, slightly bashed

a pinch of Chinese five-spice

150g bok choy, thinly sliced

150g cooked duck meat from the breast or legs, very finely sliced or shredded (or use chicken)

2 tablespoons hoisin sauce

1–2 tablespoons soy sauce

4 spring onions, finely sliced at an angle

2 tablespoons roughly chopped coriander

Place the noodles in a bowl, pour boiling water over, then leave to stand for 5 minutes, until softened. Drain and set aside, leaving about 50ml of the soaking liquid in the bowl with the noodles to stop them sticking together.

Place the stock in a saucepan over a medium heat with the ginger, garlic and the Chinese five-spice. Allow to come to the boil, then simmer with the lid on for 3 minutes. Using a slotted spoon or a sieve, remove the ginger and garlic and discard. Add the thinly sliced bok choy and cook for 1 minute, then add the duck meat and cook for another minute, until the bok choy is almost tender and the duck is hot.

Stir in the hoisin sauce and 1 tablespoon of soy sauce and taste for seasoning, adding more salty soy sauce if necessary.

To serve, divide the noodles among warm, deep, soup bowls and ladle over the soup, then scatter over the spring onions and coriander.

note *This is a great last-minute recipe, with most of it best done just before serving. But if you do want to get ahead, you could make the soup up to the point just before adding the bok choy and duck, then keep the spiced stock in the fridge for up to 2 days. The noodles can also be cooked an hour or two before they're needed, if you like.*

Pho bo – Vietnamese beef broth with rice noodles

Serves 8–10

Like ramen is to the Japanese, pho is an integral part of Vietnamese culture and cuisine. A restorative broth with noodles and beef, it's thought that it was the French, while occupying Vietnam from the 1880s to the mid 1950s, who first slaughtered beef for food. Up until then, cows had only been used as draft animals. The leftover bones and lesser cuts were made into broth and sold by street-food vendors.

Pho with chicken, *pho ga*, came about later on, perhaps some time in the late 1930s or early 1940s, when, in order to control the number of cows slaughtered, the sale of beef was forbidden on certain days.

I always make a big batch of this stock, as there's the same amount of work involved whether you're making it for 2 or for 10. The stock will keep in the fridge for a week or more, and it can be frozen too, then reheated and turned into the magical pho with the addition of noodles, shredded beef, fish sauce, lime juice, onions, chillies and herbs.

For the stock

1kg beef shin bones, sawn into pieces

1kg piece of beef brisket, trimmed of fat

50g piece of fresh ginger, sliced

1 x 6cm piece of cassia or cinnamon

2 star anise

2 teaspoons salt

To serve

75ml Vietnamese or Thai fish sauce (nam pla)

2 tablespoons freshly chopped coriander (leaves and fine stalks)

400–500g flat rice noodles (banh pho) (50g per person)

8 spring onions, sliced thinly at an angle

1 small shallot, thinly sliced

2 red chillies, thinly sliced

a small handful of Asian basil leaves, if possible, or some small Italian basil leaves, shredded

a small handful of coriander leaves

a small handful of small mint leaves, sliced

8–10 lime wedges

Place all the stock ingredients in a large saucepan, add 6 litres of water, and bring to the boil. Skim off any scum that rises to the surface, then lower the heat and simmer gently, uncovered, for 3 hours.

Remove the brisket from the stock and set it aside, or place it in the fridge once it's cool if you're serving the soup later or the next day. Strain the stock and allow it to cool. If you can, chill the strained stock in the fridge so that the fat on top will solidify, making it easier to remove. Either way, skim off any fat from the surface of the cooled stock. If the stock has any sediment from the beef it will be cloudy, and you want it to be lovely and clear. To clarify it, place a piece of kitchen paper in a sieve over a bowl and pour the stock through the sieve. What comes through will be clear and glossy.

When you want to serve the pho, pour the stock into a saucepan and bring it to the boil.

Add the fish sauce and the chopped coriander. Taste and add more fish sauce if necessary. Tear the beef along the grain of the meat into long, fine shreds.

Place the rice noodles in a bowl and cover with plenty of boiling water. Allow to sit for a few minutes, according to the instructions on the packet (or just 15 seconds if they are fresh rice noodles), until they are almost tender. Don't let them get too soft or they will be mushy by the time you eat them. Drain the noodles and divide them among deep soup bowls.

Top each bowl of noodles with a small handful of the shredded beef. Pour over the hot stock and scatter over some sliced spring onions and shallots, sliced chillies, and finally the basil, coriander and mint. Serve with a wedge of lime and chopsticks.

Dal shorba

This deliciously spicy and comforting lentil soup gets its name from the Indian word for dried split pulses, *dal*, and the Arabic word for soup, *shorba*. The lentils don't need to be pre-soaked, and take only about 10–15 minutes to cook. They need to be completely tender and rendered down to a mush for the best result.

Like many spicy dishes, this soup is just as divine reheated the next day, and it can also be frozen for batch cooking. I love to serve it with paratha (see page 260) or naan breads (see page 254).

250g red lentils

1.5 litres vegetable or chicken stock (see pages 277, 264)

1 teaspoon ground cumin

1 teaspoon ground turmeric

a few twists of black pepper

½ teaspoon cayenne pepper

½ teaspoon ground cardamom seeds

20 curry leaves

salt

½–1 tablespoon lemon juice

For the tadka

25g ghee or butter (or 2 tablespoons extra virgin olive oil, for vegans)

2 large cloves of garlic, finely chopped

2 teaspoons black mustard seeds

1 tablespoon finely chopped coriander leaves

Wash the lentils in a sieve under cold running water, then drain. Pour the stock into a saucepan and add the drained lentils, cumin, turmeric, a few twists of black pepper, the cayenne, cardamom and curry leaves. Place over a medium heat and cook for about 15 minutes, until there's absolutely no bite left in the lentils. Season with a little salt to taste. Blend the soup for just about 10 seconds, so that it becomes slightly creamy but not totally smooth. Set aside.

Now make the tadka (this is the tempering of the soup). Place a frying pan over a high heat and, once hot, add the ghee, butter or oil. Add the chopped garlic and cook until it just starts to colour, then tip in the mustard seeds and cook for another 30–60 seconds, until the garlic is golden and the mustard seeds are starting to pop (if there's any moisture in the seeds they won't pop, but don't worry, as long as they get to cook with the garlic).

Add the chopped coriander and cook for 5 seconds, then pour the tadka over the soup in the pot. Simmer together for a couple of minutes to let the flavours mingle, then add a little lemon juice and perhaps more salt to taste. Serve in deep, warm bowls.

West African peanut soup

Serves 4–6

A reassuringly simple and delicious meal-in-a-bowl, this chunky soup takes its inspiration from the West African groundnut (peanut) soup. Peanut butter gives the soup a gloriously creamy texture. I have also successfully made this soup with rice, instead of the chickpeas used here. Just add 50g of uncooked brown or white rice with the tomatoes, and cook for about 20 minutes, until the rice is tender.

2 tablespoons extra virgin olive oil

1 onion, finely chopped

2 cloves of garlic, finely chopped

2 teaspoons toasted and ground cumin (see note)

1 pinch of chilli flakes or ½ a red chilli, deseeded and finely chopped

1 large red pepper, deseeded and finely diced

1 small sweet potato, peeled and diced

salt and freshly ground pepper

1 x 400g tin of tomatoes or 400g fresh ripe tomatoes, peeled (see page 76) and chopped

1 teaspoon sugar

1 x 400g tin of chickpeas, drained (see note)

750ml vegetable or chicken stock (see pages 277, 264)

100g kale (weight without stalks)

100g chunky peanut butter

To serve

50g salted peanuts, chopped

Place a large saucepan on a medium heat and add the olive oil. Tip in the onion, garlic, cumin, chilli, red pepper and sweet potato. Season with salt and pepper and cook, uncovered, for about 10–15 minutes, until the onion is tender and a little golden around the edges.

Now add the tomatoes and any juice, the sugar, drained chickpeas and the stock. Season again with salt and pepper and cook, covered with a lid, for about 20 minutes, until all the vegetables are tender.

While the vegetables are cooking, remove the stalks from the kale and discard, then chop the leaves. Add the chopped kale to the soup when you're almost ready to serve, and cook, uncovered, for 3–4 minutes. Stir in the peanut butter and taste for seasoning.

To serve, pour the steaming hot soup into warm bowls and scatter chopped salted peanuts over the top.

 notes   *You can use 125g dried chickpeas instead of a 400g tin. Pre-soak in plenty of cold water for 5 hours or overnight, then drain and place in a saucepan with fresh cold water to cover. Bring to the boil and cook for approximately 45 minutes, until tender.*

For the best flavour, toast and grind whole cumin seeds. Place 2 teaspoons of seeds in a frying pan over a medium to high heat and cook, tossing regularly, for a couple of minutes until they're a couple of shades darker and beginning to smell aromatic. Tip them out of the pan and grind them, using a pestle and mortar or a spice grinder.

Shrimp and pork wonton soup

Probably one of my favourite recipes in this book, I absolutely adore these Chinese flavours, with the perfect balance of meat, shellfish, soy, sesame and coriander. It's a soup that is both uplifting and soothing at the same time.

I love it when I have wontons already made in the freezer, as everything else is very quick to prepare. This wonton filling will fill 40 wontons. The wrappers that I buy (from a brand called Happy Boy) come in 200g packs that contain 40 pastries/wrappers, so it's ideal to use the whole packet while you're going to the bother of making them at all. I like to fill all 40, then place whatever I don't use in the freezer on a parchment-lined tray until frozen. Then I'll tip them into a bag or box in the freezer until I'm ready to use them. They'll freeze well for up to 3 months.

For the wontons

2 spring onions

110g minced pork

110g raw shrimps or prawns

2 generous teaspoons finely
   grated fresh ginger

1 tablespoon soy sauce

1 teaspoon toasted sesame oil

2 teaspoons cornflour

40 wonton wrappers

For the soup

1 litre Asian chicken stock
   (see page 268)

2 spring onions

1 teaspoon toasted sesame oil

salt and white pepper

To serve

3 spring onions, sliced very thinly
   at an angle

a small handful of coriander leaves

a drizzle of sesame garlic chilli sauce
   (see page 206), if you like

First, make the wonton filling. Slice the spring onions very finely, then chop well. Place in a bowl and mix with the minced pork. Chop the raw shrimps or prawns until very fine – they should be as fine as the minced pork. Add to the bowl and mix with the pork, then mix in the ginger, soy sauce and sesame oil. Sift over the cornflour and mix well to combine. Fry a tiny piece of the filling in a pan to taste it for seasoning, adding a little more soy sauce if you want.

Lay the wonton wrappers out on your work surface with one of the longer sides closest to you, and the shorter sides to your left and right. Place a pastry brush in a small jug of cold water. Place 1 scant teaspoon of the filling in the centre of each wonton wrapper, then brush some water all round the pastry – I normally do this a few at a time, so the water doesn't have a chance to dry out if it's sitting for a long time. Fold the pastry rectangle away from you, pushing all air pockets out to the edges. You should now have a long rectangle with the filling inside. Grasp the bottom corners of the rectangle (the filling side, not the seam side), and dab one of the corners with a little water. Bring the two corners together, and squeeze them to seal. As you make each one, place it on a tray lined with parchment paper. When you're finished, you can chill or freeze the wontons if you wish, or cook them straight away.

To make the broth, put the stock into a saucepan with the spring onions, cut in half. Bring to the boil, then set aside to infuse while you cook the wontons.

Cook the wontons in a pan of boiling water over a medium to high heat with a good pinch of salt for 5 minutes. The pastry should be tender and the filling cooked inside.

Add the sesame oil to the stock, remove the spring onion pieces and season the stock with salt and white pepper. Pour the stock into deep bowls and add about 5 cooked wontons per person. Scatter the spring onion slices and coriander leaves over the top, and, if you wish, add a drizzle of the sesame garlic chilli sauce.

Beef and stout soup with herb and cheese dumplings

Serves 4

This is a big soup for a blustery day or for when you are in need of a hug. The deep malted flavour of stout complements beef gorgeously, though if you wish you can use all stock and no stout and it will still be great. The dumplings, which are made like a traditional Irish soda bread, soak up lots of flavour and juices, and transform this soup into a meal in a bowl. If there are any nice chunks of fat that you've removed from the beef, you can render these in the pot over a low heat (or in the preheated oven in an ovenproof dish) to use instead of the olive oil.

75g rindless streaky bacon, cut into lardons

375g trimmed stewing beef, all fat removed (I like to use chuck of beef for this, from the forequarter), cut into 1cm chunks

2 tablespoons extra virgin olive oil

1 onion, thinly sliced

1 celery stalk, finely diced

1 large carrot, peeled and finely diced

1 large clove of garlic, finely chopped

salt and freshly ground pepper

3 sprigs of thyme

1 tablespoon tomato purée

1 teaspoon sugar

500ml stout

600ml beef or chicken stock (see pages 270, 264)

For the herb and cheese dumplings

225g plain flour

½ teaspoon bicarbonate of soda

½ teaspoon salt

1 teaspoon chopped thyme

2 teaspoons chopped parsley

200–225ml buttermilk

50g finely grated cheese, such as Cheddar or Gruyére

To serve

1 tablespoon chopped parsley

Preheat the oven to 150°C/130°C fan/gas 2. Place a casserole pot or an ovenproof saucepan on a low to medium heat and immediately add the bacon – there's no need to preheat the pot, as you want the bacon to cook really slowly so that the fat renders out, leaving you with delicious crispy lardons.

When the bacon is golden and crisp, take it out, leaving all the fat in the pan, and turn the heat up to high. Once the pot is good and hot, add the beef, or just half of it if the pot is not large and you need to cook it in two batches, as the beef should be just in a single layer. If the beef dries out while you're browning it, you will need to add a

▶

drizzle of olive oil. If the pot is not hot enough, the beef may start to stew and get juicy, in which case, keep cooking it until the juices evaporate and the beef browns. Cook the beef over a light heat until it's browned all over, then take it out and cook the second batch, if you're cooking it in two batches.

Once the beef is browned, take it out and put it with the bacon. Drizzle some olive oil into the pot, then tip in the onion, celery and carrot and cook them over a high heat for a few minutes, until they start to get a little golden around the edges. Stir in the garlic and cook for a minute more, seasoning with salt and pepper.

Tip the browned bacon and beef into the vegetables and add the thyme sprigs, tomato purée, sugar, stout and stock. Bring to a simmer, then cover and place in the preheated oven for 1 hour 15 minutes. Now take the pot out of the oven and turn the heat up to 220°C/200°C fan/gas 7.

To make the dumplings, sift the flour and bicarbonate of soda into a mixing bowl and add the salt and chopped herbs. Mix together, then make a well in the centre. Pour in the buttermilk, then, with your hand in a firm claw-like position, move it around in circles, drawing the buttermilk into the flour to create a soft dough. You may need to add more buttermilk if necessary.

Once the dough comes together, tip it on to a floured worktop and dust the top with flour. Turn it and pat it until it's just 2cm thick, then cut it into about 16 small rounds, using a cutter with approximately 3cm diameter.

Take the lid off the saucepan or casserole pot and arrange the dumplings straight away on top of the soup (don't worry if they sink a little). Scatter the grated cheese on top, then put the pot back into the hot oven and bake for 20–30 minutes, until the dumplings are golden and cooked through – you might need to take one out and cut into it to check.

Take the pot out of the oven, remove the thyme sprigs and season the soup to taste. This is great just as it is, served with chopped parsley over the top, or with gremolata (see page 153), which is also lovely over this.

Serve the soup in warm bowls, with 3–4 dumplings per bowl.

 note *For a dairy-free version, you can use a plant-based milk instead of buttermilk and add 1 tablespoon of vinegar. Omit the cheese.*

South East Asian-style pork noodle soup with chilli and coriander

Serves 4–6

I adore the balance of salty, sharp, spicy and sweet flavours that is found in so much South East Asian food, like this noodle soup. The base is a flavourful broth in its own right, lovely on its own, or with noodles and perhaps some chicken or shrimps. But for a downright delicious addition, these gingery pork meatballs transform this soup into something substantial yet still light and soothing.

100g medium or fine rice noodles

For the soup

1 litre chicken stock (see page 264)

1 stalk of lemongrass, bashed (or rolled with a rolling pin) and cut in half

1 x 3cm piece of fresh ginger, cut into thin slices

juice of 1 lime

2–4 tablespoons fish sauce (nam pla)

2 teaspoons palm sugar or brown sugar

1–2 red chillies, sliced

For the pork meatballs

1 bunch of coriander, about 20 stalks

400g minced pork (not too fatty)

2 teaspoons finely grated fresh ginger

1 clove of garlic, crushed or finely grated

½–1 red chilli, finely chopped (deseeded if you wish) (optional)

salt

2 tablespoons olive oil

Place the noodles in a bowl, pour boiling water over to cover, and leave to stand for 5 minutes, until softened. Drain and set aside, leaving about 50ml of the soaking liquid with the noodles to prevent them sticking.

Place the stock, lemongrass and ginger in a saucepan and put on a high heat. Bring to the boil, then reduce the heat to medium and simmer for 5 minutes. Take the broth off the heat and add the lime juice, 2 tablespoons of the fish sauce, the sugar and most of the sliced chillies. Taste and add a splash more fish sauce or lime juice if necessary.

While the broth is simmering, cut off the thick stems from the base of the coriander stalks, just 2–3cm, and discard (or put them into your stockpot, see page 264). Pick the leaves off the remaining stems and set aside, then finely chop the stems. Mix together the minced pork, ginger, garlic, finely chopped coriander stems and the chopped chilli (if using) and season with salt. To check the mixture for seasoning, cook a little piece in a frying pan, and adjust if necessary.

▶

Roll the mixture into 20 balls. Place a large frying pan on a high heat, allow to get hot, then add the olive oil. Tip in the pork balls (if the frying pan doesn't fit them all comfortably in a single layer, cook them in two batches). Cook, stirring occasionally, for 6–8 minutes, until golden brown and cooked in the centre, then remove to a plate lined with a piece of kitchen paper.

Divide the noodles among deep, warm bowls, then add the pork balls and pour over the broth, leaving the ginger slices and lemongrass behind. Garnish with the reserved coriander leaves and the rest of the sliced chillies.

note   *You can make the pork balls ahead of time and keep them either in the fridge for up to 2 days or in the freezer for up to 3 months. Allow them to thaw before cooking.*

Creamy pork and macaroni soup

Serves 6

This soup encompasses some of my favourite comfort foods all in one big bowl. Delicious pork meatballs served in a creamy soup with macaroni and lots of grated cheese. It's a real favourite in our house.

For the meatballs
450g minced pork
175g soft breadcrumbs
1 egg, whisked
a pinch of ground nutmeg
salt and freshly ground pepper

For the soup
25g butter
1 onion, finely chopped

3 cloves of garlic, crushed or finely grated
1 tablespoon plain flour
1 litre chicken stock (see page 264)
250ml cream (regular or double)
1–2 teaspoons Dijon mustard
125g macaroni pasta

To serve
1 tablespoon chopped parsley
finely grated Parmesan

To make the meatballs, place the minced pork in a bowl, add the breadcrumbs and the egg, and mix well. Season with nutmeg, salt and pepper. Taste the mixture for seasoning by cooking a teaspoonful in a frying pan with a tiny drizzle of olive oil, and adjust if necessary. Roll the mixture into small meatballs, just about 1.5cm in diameter. Set aside in the fridge.

Melt the butter in a large saucepan over a medium heat and add the chopped onion and garlic. Season with salt and pepper. Cover with a butter wrapper or a piece of parchment paper and the saucepan lid, then turn the heat down to low and let the onions cook for about 8–10 minutes, stirring every few minutes.

Whisk the flour into the mixture, then pour on the stock while the pan is still on the heat and bring to the boil, whisking for 2 minutes while it boils to let it thicken slightly. Then pour in the cream. I like to blend the mixture at this stage to make it smooth and silky, but if you wish you can leave it as it is. Add the Dijon mustard, season with salt and pepper, and set aside.

Cook the pasta in boiling water with a large pinch of salt until just cooked, al dente.

▸

Drain, reserving all the cooking water. Stir a few tablespoons of the cooking water into the pasta to stop it sticking, and reserve the rest.

Bring the soup to the boil, then tip in the raw meatballs and bring back to the boil, stirring gently. Turn the heat down to a simmer – the meatballs will cook in the soup, giving lots of great flavour.

When the meatballs are cooked, after about 4 minutes, add the cooked pasta and a little more of the pasta cooking water if the soup needs thinning. If this soup sits around for a while, the pasta will absorb some of the liquid, so hang on to the rest of the pasta cooking water in case you need to thin it out slightly.

Serve in warm bowls, with the chopped parsley and a generous grating of Parmesan on top.

 note *The meatballs can be frozen once made, on a tray lined with parchment paper, then stored in the freezer in a box with a lid. That way, they don't stick together.*

Nduja, lentil and kale broth

Nduja, the fiery pork sausage from southern Italy, is a fabulous ingredient, which is super with meats, shellfish, eggs and vegetables. It adds its characteristic warm, intense kick to this otherwise earthy soup. Use sobrassada or chorizo if you can't get nduja.

225g Puy lentils

salt and freshly ground pepper

2 tablespoons extra virgin olive oil

225g nduja, or other spicy sausage, such as chorizo, peeled and chopped into dice or broken into chunks

1 onion, finely chopped

2 carrots, peeled and cut into 5mm dice

2 celery stalks, finely diced

2 cloves of garlic, crushed or finely grated

2 tablespoons red wine vinegar

1 tablespoon smoked paprika

1 bay leaf

1 litre chicken stock (see page 264)

225g chopped kale (weight without stalks)

2 tablespoons chopped parsley

For the paprika roasted croutons

125g bread, preferably a great sourdough or rustic white yeast, broken into 1–2cm chunks

1 teaspoon smoked paprika

sea salt flakes

2 tablespoons extra virgin olive oil

Place the lentils in a bowl. Add 1 teaspoon of salt and cover well with boiling water. Allow to stand for 30 minutes, then drain.

While the lentils are soaking, place 2 tablespoons of olive oil in a large saucepan and add the nduja. Cook over a low heat until gently browned all over. Using a slotted spoon, remove the pieces of sausage from the saucepan, leaving the oil behind, and set aside on a plate.

Add the onions, carrots, celery and garlic to the pan and season with salt and pepper. Cover and cook over a low heat, stirring every few minutes, for about 10–12 minutes, until the vegetables are tender.

Add the drained lentils, vinegar, paprika and bay leaf and cook for 2 minutes, uncovered, then pour in the stock. Cover again and simmer for 15 minutes, until the lentils are tender, then tip the nduja back into the pot with the chopped kale. Cook, uncovered, for 5 minutes, until the kale has wilted and become tender.

To make the croutons, while the soup is cooking preheat the oven to 220°C/200°C fan/gas 7. Place the bread chunks in a bowl and add the smoked paprika and a good pinch of sea salt flakes. Drizzle in the olive oil and toss to coat the bread. Tip the bread and all the paprika oil on to a roasting or baking tray and cook in the oven for 6–8 minutes, until golden and crisp.

When the soup is ready, take the saucepan off the heat, taste for seasoning, adding a splash more vinegar or more salt and pepper if it needs it, and serve in deep bowls, with a few smoked paprika roasted croutons over the top and a sprinkling of parsley.

Cambodian beef laksa

This delicious big bowl of goodness takes its inspiration from the Khmer cuisine in Cambodia. While still containing the hot, salty, sweet and sour flavours of South East Asia, Cambodian food often gets its heat from the peppercorns that have been grown there for many centuries, rather than from chillies. This laksa, or curry soup, also has a nice helping of cardamom in it, as a nod to the spice that grows in the aptly named Cardamom Mountains in the south-west of the country. Fermented shrimp paste, or *kapi* as it's called in Cambodia, and fish sauce, *tuek trey*, both feature widely in Khmer food, bringing the fifth taste – umami, which is sometimes called the meaty or mouth-filling element. A truly restorative and satisfying soup.

For the stock
300g beef brisket, in one piece
½ teaspoon whole black peppercorns
1 pandan leaf (frozen is fine)
2 whole unpeeled garlic cloves, bashed with the base a saucepan
1 cinnamon stick, 10cm long

For the paste
1 teaspoon whole cumin seeds
½ teaspoon cardamom seeds (from green cardamom pods)
½ teaspoon whole black peppercorns
3 whole cloves
50g roughly chopped shallots
25g coriander stalks (and roots if you have them), chopped

1 stalk lemongrass
1 clove of garlic, peeled
1 teaspoon finely chopped peeled fresh ginger
1 teaspoon kapi (shrimp paste)
2 tablespoons fish sauce
1 tablespoon olive oil

For the broth
1 tablespoon olive oil
1 x 400ml tin of coconut milk
3–5 tablespoons fish sauce

To finish
300g thin rice noodles
a handful of coriander leaves
crispy fried shallots (see page 202)
4 wedges of lime

Place the piece of beef in a saucepan with the whole black peppercorns, the pandan leaf, the bashed garlic cloves and the cinnamon stick. Pour over 2 litres of cold water and place the pan over a medium to high heat. Bring to the boil, then turn the heat down and allow the liquid to simmer for 1½–2 hours, until the beef is completely tender. Cover with a lid for the first hour, then cook uncovered for the remaining time.

While the stock is cooking, prepare the paste. Place the cumin, cardamom, peppercorns and cloves in a dry frying pan over a high heat. Toss regularly for about 1–2 minutes, until the spices get a bit toasted and fragrant – don't let them burn. Tip the spices into a mortar and grind with the pestle, or use a spice grinder.

Place the spices in a food processor or blender and add the shallots and coriander stalks, and the roots if using them. Trim the base and the green tops from the lemongrass and peel off the outer leaf (I like to put these into a teapot with the ginger peelings, top up with boiling water, then let it steep for 5 minutes for a really refreshing tea), then finely slice the lemongrass and add to the shallots. Add the garlic, ginger, shrimp paste, fish sauce and olive oil. Blend to a paste, scraping down the sides of the blender or food processor a few times.

When the beef is tender, the flavour of the stock should be lovely. Strain (setting the beef aside), and measure the liquid. You want 1.5 litres. Top up with a little water if you have less, or, if you have too much, pour it back into the saucepan and continue to boil, uncovered, until it's reduced to the correct amount.

Place a saucepan (one that will hold all the stock and the coconut milk) over a medium to high heat. Add a tablespoon of olive oil and then the paste. Cook the paste, stirring constantly for a few minutes, until the raw aroma from the shallots has gone and the paste has thickened slightly. Now add the coconut milk and the 1.5 litres of stock, bring to the boil and boil for 2 minutes. Season to taste with the fish sauce.

Place the noodles in a bowl and cover with boiling water. Allow to soak for 5 minutes, or until tender. Drain the noodles, keeping a couple of tablespoons of the soaking water in the bowl with them, to prevent them sticking. Slice or shred the cooked beef really thinly.

Divide the noodles among bowls and pour over the hot broth. Top with the shredded beef, coriander leaves, crispy fried shallots and a wedge of lime.

 note *If I've made this ahead of time and want to reheat the beef for the laksa, I cook it in a small drizzle of olive oil in a frying pan over a high heat, adding ½ tablespoon of fish sauce at the end. While not traditional or authentic, it is absolutely delicious like this . . .*

Garlic soup

So many countries have a garlic soup among the traditional recipes that make up the backbone of their cuisine, and this simple but divine example is so much more than the sum of its parts. The liaison, made with egg yolks and olive oil, emulsifies with the broth, giving the soup a velvety smoothness. If you want to prepare the soup in advance, only make it up to the point of adding the liaison, and avoid boiling it after the liaison has been added, to keep it lovely and silky.

For the broth

1 litre chicken stock (see page 264)

1 head of garlic, cloves separated (not peeled) and bashed with a rolling pin

2 teaspoons sea salt

a pinch of freshly ground pepper

a sprig of rosemary

2 large sprigs of parsley

For the croutons

2 tablespoons extra virgin olive oil

2 slices of white bread, crusts removed and cut into roughly 1cm cubes

For the liaison

2 egg yolks

50ml extra virgin olive oil

To serve

a drizzling of extra virgin olive oil

Place the chicken stock and the garlic cloves in a large saucepan and add the salt, pepper, rosemary and parsley. Place on a medium heat and bring to a simmer, then cover with the saucepan lid and cook gently for 30–45 minutes, until the garlic is soft. Pour the soup through a sieve into a large bowl and push the soft garlic through. Discard the skins and the herbs, then return the liquid to the saucepan, season to taste and keep warm while you make the croutons and liaison.

To make the croutons, place a frying pan on a medium-high heat, drizzle with the olive oil, then add the cubes of bread and cook, tossing frequently, for a few minutes until golden and crisp. Tip out on to a plate lined with kitchen paper and set aside.

Next, make the liaison. Place the egg yolks in a large, warmed serving bowl (not hot, or the egg yolks will scramble). Whisk for a few seconds, then continue to whisk, adding the oil in a very thin stream so that it emulsifies. Now pour the hot soup on to the liaison, whisking all the time. Divide among bowls, and add a few croutons and a small drizzle of olive oil to each one.

Beef consommé

Serves 4–6

This classic French clear soup is one that is taught in chef schools all around the world. It's such an exquisite soup, and deeply nutritious too, and is easy to master once you understand the basic concepts behind making it, and how a clarification raft works.

Basically, beef consommé is an enriched beef stock that has been clarified using egg whites. As the consommé simmers, the egg whites slowly set in the heat and form a raft that clarifies the soup – a bit of care, attention and patience is needed to make a really good consommé.

If you buy a shin of beef cut into pieces, you can use the bones to make a rich beef stock and then use the meat to flavour the consommé. In this recipe I call for the meat and vegetables to be diced by hand, but if you have a mincer, you can put the roughly chopped trimmed meat and vegetables in together and mince them quite quickly.

The beef stock that you're using to make the consommé should be as clear as possible and totally free of fat, as the fat will prevent clarification. Strain the stock, then chill it and lift any residual fat from the top for the best result.

Consommé can be served with a simple garnish of a sprig of chervil or some very small flat-leaf parsley leaves, or you can add some cooked vegetables cut into brunoise (very small dice) or julienne (small matchstick shapes). I love serving little pork, rosemary and garlic dumplings (see page 206) in the consommé.

The consommé (without the dumplings) can also be served cold, in which case it's called *consommé en gelée*. It will have the texture of a softly set jelly and is really refreshing on a summer's day. Serve straight from the fridge, in small bowls.

(GF)

350g boneless shin of beef, finely chopped and free of any fat

1 carrot, finely chopped

1 leek, finely chopped

2 celery stalks, finely chopped

2 ripe tomatoes, quartered and deseeded

3 egg whites

1.75 litres beef stock

salt and freshly ground pepper

2 tablespoons medium or dry sherry

Place the diced beef, carrots, leeks, celery and tomatoes in a large saucepan. Add the egg whites (no need to whisk them first) and the cold stock, and season with salt and pepper. Place the pot on a low heat and bring the mixture to the boil, whisking constantly.

This stage should take about 10–15 minutes. Once the mixture looks cloudy and murky, stop whisking. Keep the heat low. The egg whites will slowly cook and coagulate, forming a raft that will rise slowly to the top of the pan. Do not stir the consommé while it's cooking, as the egg white raft, if undisturbed, will filter and clarify the broth, giving you a sparkling clear consommé. Allow it to simmer gently for 1 hour to extract the flavour from the beef and vegetables. When 1 hour is up, taste the meat and vegetables and if they are a bit bland, and the broth is flavoursome, that's good.

Place a sheet of kitchen paper in a sieve over a bowl (this will help to strain and clarify the consommé broth), or use a jelly bag, and gently ladle the consommé into it, being careful to disturb the crust as little as possible. Do not press the solids in the strainer or the consommé will not be sparkling clear. Strain it a second time if necessary.

Pour the consommé into a clean saucepan, add the sherry, and season with a little more salt if necessary. Reheat the consommé, and serve.

 note *After the consommé is made, cover the leftover meat and vegetables with cold water and simmer gently for 2 hours to extract every last bit of flavour and goodness from them, then strain. This will give you a light beef stock.*

Creamy cabbage and bay leaf soup

Serves 4–6

This is a simple soup but nonetheless absolutely delicious. When cabbage is shredded or chopped and cooked quickly, it delivers a peppery sweetness that works so well in soups and is a far cry from the strong and pungent over-cooked alternative. I love to use a verdant green cabbage for this, such as the wrinkly Savoy. Of course kale can be used too. It's another soup that freezes very well.

(V)
(GF)

50g butter
150g peeled and diced potatoes
125g peeled and diced onions
1 large or 2 small bay leaves, preferably fresh

salt and freshly ground pepper
1 litre vegetable or chicken stock (see pages 277, 264)
255g chopped green cabbage (core removed)
75–100ml cream (regular or double)

Melt the butter in a saucepan over a medium heat. When it foams, add the potatoes, onions and bay leaf, season with salt and pepper, and stir. Cover with a butter wrapper or a piece of parchment paper, then turn the heat down to low, cover with the lid and cook on a gentle heat for 10 minutes, stirring every few minutes to prevent the vegetables sticking and burning.

Add the stock and boil gently, covered, until the potatoes are tender. Add the chopped cabbage and cook with the lid off until it is just tender – depending on the variety of cabbage you're using, this can take anything from 2–6 minutes. Do not overcook or the cabbage will lose its fresh flavour and green colour.

Remove the bay leaf and blend the soup with the cream in a liquidizer or blender. Taste for seasoning and serve. I love this soup with croutons scattered over the top (see page 188).

note   *If the soup is to be reheated, bring it just to steaming point and serve. Prolonged boiling spoils the colour and flavour of green soups and also this soup's smooth, silky texture.*

GARNISHES AND ACCOMPANIMENTS

Croutons

This is a really simple crouton recipe to go with any soup. Throughout the book you'll also find a few other types, such as aïoli croutons (see page 90), paprika (see page 176) and za'atar (see page 36) if you feel like something fancier.

Serves 4–6

2–3 slices of delicious white bread or sourdough
2 tablespoons extra virgin olive oil

Preheat the grill to high. Slice the crusts from the bread and discard. Cut the bread into 3cm chunks and toss them in a bowl with the olive oil. Tip on to a baking tray, spreading the croutons out in a single layer, and place under the grill for 2–3 minutes, turning them and giving the tray a shake halfway through, until the croutons are golden brown.

Croûtes

These thin, crisp croûtes are great served with soup or a salad, or topped with something delicious. The baguette needs to be a bit stale in order to slice it very thinly. A frozen baguette will also work, but you'll need a very sharp knife. I normally slice it on a tea towel if it's frozen, to stop it from slipping.

Makes about 20

½ a baguette, a few days old

Preheat the oven to 150°C/130°C fan/gas 2. Cut the bread into very thin slices at an angle, just 3–4mm if possible. Place in a single layer on a baking tray and cook for 15–20 minutes, or until crisp on both sides. Stored in an airtight box, these will keep well for a week or so.

Rosemary and olive oil croûtes

These croûtes have a sunny Mediterranean flavour. While they are best made on the day of eating, if you have any left over you can store them in a covered box for a few days. Re-warm them briefly in the oven or in a pan.

Makes about 20

50ml extra virgin olive oil
2 teaspoons finely chopped rosemary
½ a baguette, a few days old
salt

Preheat the oven to 150°C/ 130°C fan/gas 2. Place the olive oil and chopped rosemary in a small saucepan on a medium heat, bring to a gentle simmer, then turn off. Allow to sit for 10 minutes for the rosemary to infuse the oil.

Cut the bread into very thin slices at an angle, just 3–4 mm if possible. Place in a single layer on a baking tray and brush the rosemary oil over the slices, just on one side, then sprinkle with a little salt. Cook in the preheated oven for 15–20 minutes, or until crisp on both sides. Store in an airtight box.

Toasted pitta wedges

These are great for serving with soup, and also for dipping into and scooping up hummus, guacamole and pâté.

Serves approximately 6

3 pitta breads

3 tablespoons extra virgin olive oil

a good pinch of sea salt flakes

1 teaspoon cumin seeds, toasted and crushed or ground

Preheat the oven to 220°C/200°C fan/gas 7. Cut the pitta bread into wedges or strips, put them into a bowl, toss with the olive oil to coat, then add the sea salt and crushed cumin. Spread out flat on a baking tray and cook for about 5 minutes, or until light golden.

Tortilla chips

Making your own tortilla chips, called *totopos* in Mexico, is a game-changer. Speedy to prepare and super delicious, they are great served with Mexican-style soups, or of course make a delicious snack for dipping. Use corn or wheat tortillas, and if you fancy, toss them in finely grated hard cheese (such as Parmesan) with a pinch of cayenne pepper for a nice little kick.

6 corn or wheat flour tortillas

oil, for deep frying

salt

Cut the tortillas into wedges.

Heat the oil to 200°C and fry the tortilla wedges until light golden, stirring occasionally to ensure that they brown evenly. Drain on kitchen paper and toss with some salt.

Roasted garlic soldiers (V)

This recipe will make an army's worth of soldiers. But if you prefer, you can halve the recipe, or just freeze whatever you don't need – then bake them another time.

Serves 8

175g butter

6–8 cloves of garlic, crushed or finely grated

2 tablespoons chopped parsley

1 baguette

Preheat the oven to 230°C/210°C fan/gas 8. In a saucepan, melt the butter until foaming, then add the garlic and parsley.

Split the baguette in two lengthwise and generously brush the garlic butter over the cut sides, using it all. On a chopping board, cut each length into 2cm slices. Arrange the soldiers on a baking tray and bake in the hot oven for 6–8 minutes, or until toasted and golden brown. Use straight away, or freeze for another time.

Halloumi croutons

Technically not croutons at all, as they're not made of bread, but these are a delicious alternative and great scattered over Middle Eastern-style soups, such as the carrot and harissa (see page 36), or many others too . . .

Serves 4–6

2 tablespoons extra virgin olive oil
150g halloumi, cut into 1.5cm dice

Place a frying pan over a medium heat with a drizzle of the olive oil. Pat the halloumi dice dry with kitchen paper, then place in a single layer in the pan. Cook on one side until golden, then gently toss to cook on another side, continuing to turn until the halloumi is golden all over. Transfer to a plate lined with kitchen paper, then scatter over hot soup.

Chorizo crumbs

These crispy little nuggets of deliciousness are great scattered over green soups, or root vegetable soups, like potato, Jerusalem artichoke and celeriac. They're also super scattered over fish pie or cauliflower cheese.

Serves 6–8

4 tablespoons extra virgin olive oil
125g chorizo, peeled and cut into 5mm dice
100g slightly coarse breadcrumbs

Place the olive oil in a cool pan and add the chorizo. Toss on a low heat until the oil starts to run and the chorizo begins to crisp. Beware – if the heat is too high it's easy to burn the chorizo. Drain through a metal sieve, saving the oil, and return the oil to the pan.

Increase the heat to medium-high. Add the breadcrumbs and stir constantly in the oil until crisp and golden, about 2–3 minutes. Drain, then add the crumbs to the chorizo pieces.

These keep well in a covered box in the fridge for a few days. Reheat in a hot pan for a few minutes before scattering them over a soup.

Seed crackers

My friend Susan regularly makes these crackers to enjoy with soup, cheese or charcuterie. Gluten-free, they keep well for weeks. They are delicious just like this, or great with a teaspoon or two of cumin seeds, fennel seeds, smoked paprika or chopped rosemary or thyme added to the mix or even sprinkled on top before baking. The half-cup of chia seeds or ground flaxseeds is very important, as this is the 'glue' that sticks them together. Make sure you use the same size cup for measuring everything, as it's all about the ratio of ingredients.

Makes about 40

a little olive oil or coconut oil
1½ cups (whatever size) of mixed seeds such as
     sesame, sunflower, poppy, pumpkin seeds

½ a cup of chia seeds, or ground flaxseeds
  (I grind these in my blender), or a mixture
a good pinch of salt
1 cup of water

Preheat the oven to 170°C/150°C fan/gas 3.
Line a large baking tray with parchment paper
and grease with olive oil or coconut oil.

Place the mixed seeds in a large bowl. Stir in
the chia or ground flaxseeds, the salt and then
the water. Leave it all to sit for 10 minutes (no
longer), then, using your hands or a spatula,
spread it out to cover the parchment paper.

Bake in the preheated oven for 30 minutes,
then cut into squares or rectangles, turn them
over, and bake for about another 10 minutes,
until dry and crisp. Watch them, as they can
easily burn. (Susan suggests turning off the
oven for this final stage, so they just crisp up
slowly as the oven cools down – this works
really well. Store in an airtight box.

Pangrattato VG

Pangrattato means breadcrumbs in Italian.
Depending on the soup that I'm serving
these with, sometimes I add a small pinch
of chilli flakes, or a grating of lemon zest
and a little horseradish.

Makes 100g

50ml extra virgin olive oil
2 large cloves of garlic, peeled and bashed
50g soft, white breadcrumbs (can be frozen
  and thawed)

Place a metal sieve over a bowl. (Don't use a
plastic sieve or the hot oil will burn a hole in it.)

Heat the olive oil in a frying pan or a sauté
pan and add the garlic. Cook over a medium
heat until the garlic turns golden, then discard
(or put into a chicken stockpot). Add the
breadcrumbs to the pan and cook until crisp
and golden, then quickly pour them into
the metal sieve, saving the oil underneath for
another batch of pangrattato. Transfer to a
plate lined with kitchen paper and leave to cool.

These keep well in a covered box in the fridge
for a few days. Reheat in a hot pan for a few
minutes before scattering them over a soup.

Dukkah

An Egyptian and Middle Eastern condiment
consisting of mixed spices, herbs and
nuts, dukkah is used as a dip with fresh
vegetables, grilled meats, boiled eggs
or crusty bread, but is also a wonderful
addition to a soup.

Makes 150g

30g whole hazelnuts, with the skins on
4 tablespoons sesame seeds
2 tablespoons whole coriander seeds
2 tablespoons whole cumin seeds
2 tablespoons black peppercorns
1 teaspoon ground cinnamon
½ teaspoon salt

Preheat the oven to 180°C/160°C fan/gas 4. Put the hazelnuts on a baking tray and roast for 8–12 minutes, until the skins are starting to flake away and the nuts are golden underneath.

Tip the nuts on to a clean tea towel and rub off the skins, discarding. Put the nuts in a bowl.

While the nuts are roasting, heat a frying pan over a medium heat and add the sesame seeds. Shake the pan gently until they turn a shade darker and smell nutty. Tip into the bowl with the nuts. Repeat with the coriander and cumin seeds, together, toasting until they turn a couple of shades darker and aromatic, adding the black peppercorns for the last 10 seconds.

Place the roast spices, sesame and hazelnuts in a clean spice or coffee grinder and whiz quickly for a coarse, dry powder. Mix with the cinnamon and salt. This keeps for a few weeks in a screw-top jar.

Place the dried chillies in a bowl and cover with boiling water. Allow to sit for 30 minutes.

Meanwhile, put the cumin, coriander and caraway seeds into a dry frying pan over a medium to high heat. Toss the spices in the pan regularly, cooking until they're aromatic and a couple of shades darker. Keep a close eye on them, as they can burn very quickly. Tip the spices out of the pan and crush well using a pestle and mortar or spice grinder.

Once the chillies have softened, take them out of the water (saving the water in case you need it) and discard the stalks and seeds. Blend the chillies with the crushed toasted spices, smoked paprika, garlic and salt, then pour in the olive oil to make a thick paste, adding some of the reserved water if necessary. Taste for seasoning, adding a little more salt if necessary.

This will keep in the fridge, covered with an extra layer of olive oil, for a few months.

Harissa

A fabulously spicy and smoky North African sauce that is used as a condiment for meats, fish, vegetables and eggs, but also for bringing great depth and kick to soups.

Makes 150g

50g dried red chillies
2 teaspoons cumin seeds
1½ teaspoons coriander seeds
½ teaspoon caraway seeds
½ teaspoon smoked paprika
3 cloves of garlic, finely grated or crushed
a large pinch of salt
50ml extra virgin olive oil

Tapenade

A delicious blend of olives, capers, anchovies and olive oil, tapenade gets its name from the Provençal word for capers, *tapenas*. It can be spread on bread or served with grilled meats, and I love it on croutons or toasts served with Mediterranean-style soups.

Makes 225g

100g black olives (weight when pitted)
50g anchovies
1 tablespoon capers
1 generous teaspoon Dijon mustard
1 teaspoon lemon juice

freshly ground black pepper

50ml extra virgin olive oil

Place the pitted olives and the anchovies in a food processor or blender, and add the capers, mustard, lemon juice, a few twists of black pepper and half the olive oil. Blend until almost, but not quite, smooth, adding nearly all (but a couple of tablespoons) of the remaining olive oil. Taste for seasoning – you probably won't need any salt.

Stored in a sterilized jar and covered with a layer of olive oil (the couple of tablespoons remaining), the tapenade will keep for 6 months or so. Every time you use it, pour the olive oil into a little bowl, spoon out however much tapenade you need, then bang the jar gently but firmly on the counter to level it again and cover with the reserved olive oil. Place back in the fridge.

Aïoli

A gutsy, garlicky mayonnaise, aïoli can be made with a mayo from your fridge by adding crushed garlic and chopped parsley, or you can make it from scratch. I love liberal amounts of Dijon mustard in my aïoli too.

Makes 250g

2 egg yolks

a pinch of salt

1 teaspoon Dijon mustard

3–4 cloves of garlic, finely grated or crushed

½ tablespoon white wine vinegar

175ml tasteless oil, such as sunflower oil

50ml extra virgin olive oil

1 scant tablespoon chopped parsley

Put the egg yolks into a bowl with the salt, mustard, garlic and the white wine vinegar.

Put the oils in a jug. With a whisk in one hand and the jug in the other, drizzle the oil on to the egg yolks in a very thin, steady stream, whisking all the time. Be sure to let the oil emulsify into the egg yolks as you're whisking, i.e. don't pour the oil in too quickly or the mixture will split.

Within a minute you should notice the mixture beginning to thicken. Continue until you've used all the oil. Mix in the parsley, taste and add a little more seasoning and vinegar if necessary. Store, covered, in the fridge, for up to 1 week.

note

If the aïoli splits it will suddenly become thin and watery. To rectify this, pour the split mixture into the oil jug and place an extra egg yolk in a clean bowl. Whisking all the time, pour the split mixture on to the yolk in a very thin stream.

Zhoug

A completely delicious Yemeni, green, pesto-like sauce that's made with chilli and coriander. It's often served with falafel, grilled meats (it's divine with lamb chops), pitta and hummus, and it's also great drizzled over a steaming hot bowl of soup, such as the chunky chickpea and chorizo broth (see page 127), the beetroot and tahini soup (see page 29) or the carrot, cumin and coriander soup (see page 112). This will keep well, like a pesto. See page 196 for storing instructions.

Makes 125g

1 green chilli

2 large cloves of garlic, roughly chopped

25g fresh coriander, leaves and fine stems

½ teaspoon ground cardamom

1 teaspoon toasted and ground cumin

1–2 tablespoons lemon juice

sea salt

75ml extra virgin olive oil

Cut the top off the chilli at the stalk end, then turn the chilli upside down, shake out the seeds and discard. Chop the chilli roughly and place half of it in a food processor. Add the garlic, the coriander leaves and fine stalks, the cardamom, cumin and 1 tablespoon of lemon juice.

Blend until almost fine, then add a pinch of salt and most of the olive oil, adding the remaining chilli if you want it to be hotter. Blend again and taste for seasoning.

Tip into a bowl and drizzle with the remaining oil. Store in a jar in the fridge.

Basil pesto (V) (GF)

Making your own pesto is so worthwhile and satisfying. A little goes a very long way and is just delicious when drizzled over a chunky broth or a smooth and silky soup. Stored properly, a pesto will keep for up to a year.

Makes 150g

25g basil leaves, chopped

25g pine or cashew nuts

2 cloves of garlic, crushed or finely grated

75ml extra virgin olive oil, plus extra for the top

25g finely grated Parmesan cheese or vegetarian version

salt and freshly ground pepper

Place the basil in a food processor and add the pine or cashew nuts, and the garlic. Blend until the basil is finely puréed, then add the olive oil and blend again. Tip in the finely grated cheese and blend just to combine. Season to taste.

Pour into sterilized jars, cover with 1cm of extra virgin olive oil and cover with a lid. Stored in the fridge, unopened, the pesto will keep for up to a year. Once the jar has been opened, it will keep, if stored properly, for 3 months.

notes

Any time you want to use some pesto, pour the olive oil into a small clean bowl, spoon out some pesto, then bang the jar back down on your worktop. Clean inside the jar with kitchen paper, then pour the olive oil back over the top, cover and pop back in the fridge again.

If I'm making a big batch I store it in small jars, as once opened each jar only keeps for 3 months, rather than 1 year if it remains tightly shut.

Parsley pesto

Parsley makes a wonderfully verdant pesto for drizzling over soups and broths. Store in a sterilized jar in the fridge, always covered with a 1cm layer of olive oil. (The notes for basil pesto, page 196, also apply here.)

Makes about 150ml

25g flat-leaf or curly parsley leaves (weight once stalks removed)
25g grated Parmesan cheese or vegetarian version
25g pine nuts or cashews
1 clove of garlic, crushed
100ml extra virgin olive oil
salt

Put all the ingredients except the olive oil and salt into a food processor and blend until almost smooth. Add 75ml of the olive oil and a pinch of salt. Pour into a sterilized jar, cover with 1cm of extra virgin olive oil, using more olive oil if necessary, and store in the fridge.

Kale and hazelnut pesto

It doesn't take much kale to make a batch of pesto, and its nutty, earthy flavour works really well. I love having a jar of this in the fridge to serve with soups, stews, roasted or grilled meats, pasta, pizzas and risottos.

Makes a 400g jar

100g kale, curly kale or cavolo nero (weight without stalks), roughly chopped

60g hazelnuts, roasted and peeled (see note)
1 large clove of garlic, peeled and crushed or finely grated
250ml extra virgin olive oil
30g finely grated hard cheese, such as extra mature Coolea (Irish farmhouse cheese), Parmesan or pecorino or vegetarian version
salt

Place the chopped kale in a food processor and whiz for a couple of minutes, until quite finely chopped. Add the hazelnuts, garlic and all but 50ml of the olive oil, and blend until almost smooth. Now add the grated cheese, mix well and taste for seasoning.

Pour into a sterilized jar, banging it down on the worktop to remove any air bubbles, then cover with the remaining oil, and a lid, and store in the fridge for up to 1 year.

notes

To roast hazelnuts, cook on a tray in a moderate oven for 8–10 minutes, or until golden under the skins. Tip out on to a tea towel, then rub off and discard the skins. Cool the nuts before blending.

The notes for basil pesto, page 196, also apply.

Roasted walnut pesto

A creamier pesto than the classic green herb variety, this has a nice bite from roasted nuts. Other nuts, such as pecans, cashews and pine nuts, work well too. Not only great for soup, this is delicious stirred through pasta and risottos, and drizzled over pizza.

(The notes under basil pesto, page 196, also apply here.)

Makes a 400g jar

150g walnuts

2 cloves of garlic

salt

50g parsley leaves, stalks removed (you can use either flat-leaf or curly parsley)

125ml extra virgin olive oil

75g finely grated Parmesan or Gran Padano cheese or vegetarian version

Preheat the oven to 180°C/160°C fan/gas 4. Place the walnuts on a baking tray and roast for 10–12 minutes, until crunchy, and golden inside. Remove from the oven and allow to cool.

Crush the garlic well with a good pinch of salt. Place in a food processor or a mortar and add the cooled roasted walnuts and the parsley leaves. Blend until still just a little coarse, or pound in the mortar using the pestle, then add the olive oil and the grated cheese and pound until mixed.

Season to taste, then use straight away or place in a sterilized jar, banging it on the worktop to remove any air bubbles. Cover with a little more olive oil, and a lid, and store in the fridge for up to 1 year.

Wild garlic and almond pesto

I love the flavour of almonds with wild garlic in this springtime pesto, but if you prefer, cashews, pine nuts, walnuts, pecans, hazelnuts or macadamias can also be used.

Makes a 300g jar

50g wild garlic leaves (weight when destalked)

25g peeled (blanched) almonds (see note)

1 small clove of garlic, peeled and crushed or finely grated

225ml extra virgin olive oil

25g freshly grated Parmesan or pecorino or extra mature Coolea (a delicious Irish farmhouse cheese) or vegetarian version

salt

Blend the wild garlic with the nuts, garlic and half the olive oil in a food processor, or pound using a pestle and mortar. Add a bit more olive oil, saving a few tablespoons. Mix in the grated cheese and season to taste. Pour into a sterilized jar, bang on the worktop to remove air bubbles, then cover with the remaining oil, and a lid, and store in the fridge for up to 1 year.

notes

To blanch (peel) almonds, drop the nuts with their skins on into a small saucepan of boiling water. Boil for 1 minute, then take an almond out to test. If it pops out of its skin, they're all ready. Drain and cool slightly, then rub in a clean tea towel to remove and discard the skins. (Almonds bought with skins stay fresher for longer than ready-peeled almonds.) The notes for basil pesto, page 196, also apply here.

Rosemary oil

This heady, verdant oil is great drizzled over soups or roasted vegetables, or for barbecues or marinating lamb. It keeps for a few months, so make the full batch if you wish, or you can halve or even quarter the recipe.

Makes 100ml

100ml extra virgin olive oil
2 tablespoons chopped rosemary

Put the olive oil into a small saucepan and add the chopped rosemary. Heat until hot but not smoking. Take off the heat and allow to cool completely, then strain through a fine sieve, discarding the rosemary and keeping the oil. Decant into a small bottle with a lid if storing.

Basil oil

Basil oil adds a sunny essence of summer to soups and stews. Once made, it'll keep in the fridge for up to a month.

Makes 50ml

8–10 large basil leaves, roughly chopped
50ml extra virgin olive oil

Put the basil into a blender with the olive oil and whiz until smooth. If you don't have a blender small enough, you can use a pestle and mortar. Just pound the chopped basil well, adding a small pinch of salt for friction if you like, then add the olive oil gradually, continuing to pound until you have a rich, verdant mixture. Store in a screw-top jar in the fridge.

Fennel seed oil

This is a fragrant and flavoursome oil for drizzling over soups, for example the leek and fennel soup (see page 74).

Serves 4–6

2 teaspoons whole fennel seeds
50ml extra virgin olive oil

Grind the fennel seeds until just slightly coarse, using a spice grinder or a pestle and mortar.

Place the olive oil in a small saucepan and add the ground fennel seeds. Allow the oil to heat up, just until hot to the touch, then take off the heat and let the fennel and oil infuse for at least 20 minutes before drizzling over soup.

The fennel oil can be stored in a jar out of the fridge.

Smoked paprika oil

This vibrant red oil has a warming smokiness and looks lovely drizzled over lighter coloured soups, such as potato, cauliflower or parsnip.

Makes about 60ml

2 teaspoons smoked paprika
4 tablespoons extra virgin olive oil

Simply mix the smoked paprika with the olive oil. Store in a jar or small bottle.

Baked kale crisps

Kale leaves have a wonderful ability to crisp up really well when tossed with a little olive oil and baked in the oven. These are great as a snack or served beside or on top of soup. Curly kale, as fresh as possible, seems to work best.

Serves 1–6, depending on mood!

125g curly kale (weight without the stalks)
2 tablespoons extra virgin olive oil
sea salt flakes and a little sugar

Preheat the oven to 150°C/130C fan/gas 2.

Tear the kale leaves into large bite-size pieces. Place in a wide bowl and drizzle in the olive oil. Season with sea salt flakes and a pinch of sugar, and toss well so that each piece is dressed.

Spread out in a single layer on two baking trays and bake in the preheated oven for 20 minutes, or until crisp. Transfer to a wire rack to cool, where they'll get even more crisp.

The crisps will keep in an airtight box for a couple of days.

Crispy fried shallots

Crispy fried shallots, which are a lovely addition to so many soups, laksas, broths, curries, salads, rice and noodle dishes, can be made in advance and stored for a few days, though of course they're just divine when freshly cooked. Often bought from Asian grocers, they're so simple to make.

Serves 4

150g finely sliced shallots (you can use a mandolin if you're slicing lots)
250ml olive or sunflower oil

Once the shallots are thinly sliced, place them in a medium saucepan and cover them with the oil (which should be at room temperature). Bring to the boil and cook them until they're really bubbling – this may take a few minutes – then turn the heat down to low and cook until they start to turn a light golden brown, stirring regularly, approximately 8–10 minutes. Pay really close attention to the shallots while they're browning and do stir regularly, as they can cook unevenly or burn in patches.

While the shallots are cooking, place a metal sieve (not a plastic one, or you may burn a hole in it!) over a bowl.

Pour the shallots and oil into the sieve, draining the oil (this shallot-flavoured oil can be used again), then tip the shallots on to kitchen paper and sprinkle with salt. Store in an airtight box.

Roast red pepper, pine nut and olive salsa

This salsa packs a punch that's deliciously Moorish in flavour. I love it drizzled over soups, such as the roasted parsnip and cauliflower soup with smoked paprika (see page 133). It's divine with a few grilled lamb chops too.

Serves 6–8

1 red pepper, roasted, peeled, deseeded and cut into 5mm dice

2 tablespoons coarsely chopped green or black olives

2 tablespoons toasted pine nuts, coarsely chopped (see note)

2 tablespoons extra virgin olive oil

1 tablespoon sherry vinegar

1 teaspoon smoked paprika

salt and freshly ground pepper

Place the roasted red pepper dice in a bowl with the olives and pine nuts. Add the olive oil, sherry vinegar and smoked paprika. Season to taste with salt and pepper.

This will keep in a jar in the fridge for up to a week. Just bring it up to room temperature before drizzling it over soups.

 note

To toast pine nuts, place them in a dry frying pan over a medium to high heat, and cook them for about 3 minutes, tossing regularly, until mottled and golden brown.

Tomato and coriander salsa

Different versions of this salsa are made all across central and South America. It's served with grilled meat or fish, and of course it's also delicious as a refreshing topping on a soup. For those who dislike coriander, chopped parsley will also be good.

Serves 6–8

4 large ripe tomatoes (core removed and discarded), cut into 5mm–1cm dice

1 tablespoon finely chopped onion, or red onion

1 clove of garlic, finely grated or crushed

½–1 green or red chilli, deseeded (if you wish) and finely chopped

2 tablespoons chopped coriander

1 tablespoon extra virgin olive oil

a squeeze of lime or lemon juice

salt, freshly ground pepper and a few pinches of sugar

Place the diced tomatoes in a bowl. Add the chopped onion and the garlic, and mix well together, ensuring that the garlic gets evenly dispersed. Mix in the chilli, coriander and olive oil, and add some lime or lemon juice with salt, pepper and sugar to taste.

Serve straight away or keep for up to a couple of hours.

Sticky pork with sesame

I absolutely love this Chinese-style blend of flavours and textures. The pork is sweet, sticky, mildly spicy and downright delicious. This recipe makes enough to fill 8 bao buns, but is also fantastic without the buns, served as a little bite or starter, perhaps with some steamed bok choi too. It's also delicious served with the egg drop soup (see page 54).

Fills 8 bao buns, or can be served as a little bite or starter

1kg rindless and boneless belly of pork, cut into 8 slices, each 1cm thick

1 tablespoon olive oil

100g light brown sugar

4 cloves of garlic, sliced thinly

40g piece of fresh ginger, peeled and thinly sliced

2 whole star anise

a good pinch of Chinese five-spice

100ml Shaoxing rice wine

2 tablespoons dark soy sauce

For the toppings

1 tablespoon sesame seeds

½ a small cucumber

6 spring onions

a small handful of coriander leaves

Preheat the oven to 150°C/130°C fan/gas 2. Cut the pork belly slices in half lengthwise. Place a casserole pot or wide saucepan on a high heat and allow it to get hot, then add the olive oil and the pork slices. Cook them until they are a rich golden brown underneath, then turn them over and cook on the second side until golden. If your pot is a bit small you may have to brown the slices in batches.

When the pork is all browned, take it out of the pot and set aside on a plate. Leaving all the fat in the pot, with the heat now reduced to medium, add the brown sugar. Stir until it dissolves and becomes silky, and continue cooking and stirring until the sugar turns a couple of shades darker and caramelizes. Tip the pork and any juices from the plate back into the pot, then add the garlic, ginger, star anise, Chinese five-spice, Shaoxing rice wine and soy sauce.

Bring to a simmer, then cover with a lid and place in the preheated oven for 1 hour, by which time the pork should be tender and sticky all over. Take the pot out of the oven – if there is still a lot of juice, place the pot, uncovered, over a medium heat and allow it to bubble until the juices are thick and sticky.

While the pork is cooking, prepare the toppings. Toast the sesame seeds in a dry frying pan over a medium to high heat for a minute, until slightly darker, then tip out into a bowl.

Cut the cucumber in half lengthwise, then scoop out the seeds and cut the cucumber into slices at an angle, just 5mm thick. Cut the trimmed spring onions into thin slices at an angle.

Serve 2 slices of the pork in each of the bao buns and scatter the cucumber and spring onion slices over the top, then finish with coriander leaves and a final sprinkling of sesame seeds.

Sesame garlic chilli sauce

I love to use this sesame garlic chilli sauce on ramen, but it's divine on everything from roast meats to avocado on toast.

Makes about 125ml

25ml extra virgin olive oil or vegetable oil (I use the untraditional olive oil)

6 cloves of garlic: 4 peeled and sliced, 2 roughly chopped

75ml toasted sesame oil

2 red chillies, roughly chopped

25g sesame seeds

½ teaspoon sugar

½ teaspoon salt

Place the olive oil in a small saucepan with the 4 sliced cloves of garlic and cook over a gentle heat, stirring almost constantly, for about 8–10 minutes, until deep dark brown and very sticky.

Take off the heat, add the sesame oil and stir to mix, scraping all the garlic off the bottom of the pan. Tip into a blender (don't wash the pan yet) and blend on high speed until completely puréed, about 30 seconds. Return the mixture to the saucepan (don't wash the blender yet), and add the chillies and the 2 roughly chopped garlic cloves. Cook gently over a low heat until the chillies and garlic just begin to bubble, then remove from the heat and set aside to cool.

Grind the sesame seeds in the blender until roughly ground, then stir into the oil mixture, adding the sugar and salt. Transfer to a sealable container or jar with a lid, and store in the refrigerator for up to 2 months.

Pork, rosemary and garlic dumplings

Simple and quick little dumplings to serve in your consommé, these are delicious little meatballs. Make sure they're well seasoned for wonderful little bursts of flavour.

Serves 4–6

150g finely minced pork

1 scant teaspoon finely chopped rosemary

1 clove of garlic, finely grated or crushed

salt and freshly ground pepper

1–2 tablespoons extra virgin olive oil

Place the minced pork in a bowl with the rosemary and garlic and mix well. Season with salt and pepper. Place a frying pan on a medium heat and drizzle in a tiny bit of olive oil. Cook ½ teaspoon of the mixture in the pan, and taste for seasoning. When you're happy with the flavour, roll the mixture into small balls, not much bigger than the size of a marble.

To cook, place a frying pan over a medium heat, add a little olive oil, then tip in the dumplings and fry them until golden all over and cooked in the centre, shaking them in the pan regularly. Drain the dumplings on kitchen paper, then add them to bowls of steaming consommé.

The dumplings can be made in advance, covered and stored in the fridge overnight, or they can be frozen. To freeze, place them on a small tray lined with parchment paper and put in the freezer for a couple of hours. Then you can slide them off the tray into a box with a lid. This way, they won't stick together.

Pork and sage tortellini

Little flavoursome bundles of joy, these tortellini are wonderful served in a seasoned chicken stock for an uplifting and soothing bowl of goodness. The tortellini can be made in advance and stored in the freezer. Tray-freeze them first by placing on a parchment paper-lined tray in the freezer until frozen, then transfer to a covered box to store.

Makes 40 tortellini

For the filling
100g finely minced pork
1 clove of garlic, finely grated or crushed
1 scant teaspoon finely chopped sage
100ml cream (regular or double)
1 small egg, or ½ a large egg, whisked
salt and freshly ground pepper

For the pasta
175g '00' white flour
½ teaspoon salt
2 eggs

First, make the filling. Place the minced pork in a food processor with the garlic and sage and blend briefly to combine. Add the cream and egg, then season with salt and pepper to taste. Cook a little of this filling in a frying pan with a small drizzle of olive oil and taste for seasoning. Set the filling aside in the fridge until you're ready to use it.

Next, make the pasta. Place the flour in a bowl and add the salt. Whisk the eggs in a separate bowl. Make a well in the centre of the dry ingredients and add half the beaten egg, then rub together, using your fingertips. When it is crumbly (before you form it into a ball of dough), check to see if there is enough moisture in it by squeezing a little piece together. It should be quite dry and just able to come together. If it won't, you need to add more egg.

Knead the dough on your worktop for 10 minutes, until smooth on the outside. It should be quite difficult to knead. Cover it with an upturned bowl and leave to rest on your worktop for 20 minutes, or if you want to roll it later/tomorrow, cover and place in the fridge.

Divide the dough in half. Dust the first half with just a little '00' flour, and roll into a very thin sheet, keeping the other piece covered with the upturned bowl. I use a pasta machine, but if you have the time and patience, you can use a rolling pin. When you've rolled the first piece, keep it covered with one or two tea towels, then repeat with the second half of the dough.

Cut the pasta into 7cm circles, keeping it covered with a tea towel when you're not working with it as you don't want it to dry out. Gather the scraps into a ball and put them with the remaining pieces of dough to re-roll later.

Put some water in a small bowl next to you. Place scant teaspoonfuls of filling on to each circle, just off centre, then dip your finger in the water and run it around the edge of the circle to moisten it. Fold the circles over into half-moon shapes and press down firmly to seal the edges, pushing out any trapped air. Now hold each one and wrap it around your index finger, press the two ends firmly together to seal to resemble rounded bonnets, then slide it off your finger.

Transfer the tortellini to a tray sprinkled with a little '00' flour. Place in the fridge unless you're cooking them straight away. They can also be frozen on parchment paper – once frozen, they can be transferred to a box with a lid.

To cook the tortellini, bring a large saucepan of water to the boil with 2 teaspoons of salt added. Gently add the tortellini and cook over a high heat for 2–3 minutes, depending on how thin the pasta is, or until almost tender (al dente). By this stage the filling will be cooked. Drain, then add to a hot bowl of consommé. I like to serve about 5–7 per bowl, or 3 for a small serving.

Prawn Ravioli

You could use shrimp or lobster for this too. If you can use raw prawns, you'll get the best flavour, but cooked shellfish is next best, and still absolutely delicious. These are wonderful cooked and served floating in a bowl of bisque, but also great on a plate with some sizzling hot herb butter drizzled over the top.

Makes approximately 40 ravioli

For the filling
100g peeled raw (or cooked) prawns
100ml cream
1 small egg, or ½ a large egg, whisked
salt and freshly ground pepper

For the pasta
175g '00' white flour
½ teaspoon salt
2 eggs

First, make the filling. Place the peeled prawns in a food processor and blend until fine, then add the cream and egg. Season with salt and pepper. Set the filling aside in the fridge until you're ready to use it.

Next, make the pasta. Place the flour in a bowl and add the salt. Whisk the eggs together in a separate bowl. Make a well in the centre of the dry ingredients and add half the beaten egg, then rub together, using your fingertips. When it is at a crumbly stage (before you form it into a ball of dough), check to see if there is enough moisture in it by squeezing a little piece together. It should be quite dry and just about able to come together. If it will not stick together, you will need to add some more egg.

Knead the dough on your worktop for 10 minutes, until it becomes smooth on the outside. It should be quite difficult to knead. Cover it with an upturned bowl and leave it to rest for 20 minutes, or, if you want to roll it later, or tomorrow, cover it and place it in the fridge.

Divide the dough in half, then roll out the first half, dusting it just a little with some '00' flour, into a very thin sheet, keeping the other piece covered with the upturned bowl. I use a pasta machine for this, but if you have the time and the inclination, you can use a rolling pin. When you've rolled the first piece, keep it covered with one or two tea towels, then repeat with the second half of the dough.

Lay a sheet of dough on your worktop or a large chopping board. Whichever sheet is larger, save that one for the top. (If you've used a pasta machine they will be similar in size, about 32 x 14cm.)

Place ½ teaspoonful blobs of filling evenly down and across the pasta sheets, leaving 2.5cm intervals between. You should get about 10 down and 4 across the sheet. Now brush some water all round the edges and between every blob of filling, up and down. Lay the top sheet over the bottom sheet, making sure not to stretch it over the top or the ravioli could break while cooking. Using the outside of your hand (like a karate chop), press down on the pasta in the aisles between the blobs, going lengthwise and widthways so that the top sheet sticks to the bottom sheet, sealing around the filling of each ravioli with your fingers. You don't want too much air in the ravioli, so press out the excess to the edges if there is any.

Using a serrated pastry wheel, or just a sharp knife, cut lengthwise and widthways to make approximately 40 ravioli. Each one should be approximately 3.5cm square. Transfer to a tray sprinkled with a little '00' flour and place in the fridge, unless you're cooking them straight away. They can also be frozen on parchment paper – when frozen, transfer them to a box with a lid.

To cook the ravioli, bring a large pan of water to the boil with 2 teaspoons of salt added. Gently add the ravioli, bring back to the boil, and cook over a high heat for 2–3 minutes, depending on how thin the pasta is, or until almost tender (al dente). Drain, then place in a hot bowl of bisque. I like to serve about 5–7 ravioli per bowl.

BREAD

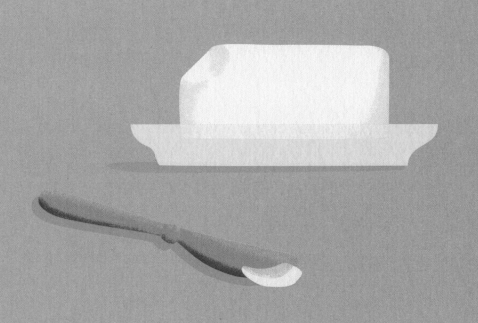

Soaked wholemeal or white bread

Makes a 2lb loaf

With more and more people becoming intolerant of the recent method of making fast-rise, sliced-pan bread, traditional bread-making methods, such as sourdough and soaked-grain breads, are becoming really popular once again.

By soaking the grains or flour with an acidic ingredient such as vinegar, lemon juice, whey, yoghurt or buttermilk, the phytates in the grain (which can make regular bread difficult to digest, and the nutrients hard to absorb) break down, reducing the amount of phytic acid.

In the making of a sourdough bread, the presence of wild yeast and lactobacillus neutralizes the phytic acid as the bread proves, through the acidification of the dough.

Here I have made both a wholemeal bread and a white bread using this soaking method. In the recipe I recommend soaking the flour for 24 hours. This is not a sourdough, but if you are looking for a slight sour tang from your bread, you can soak it for 48 hours.

For the wholemeal bread
225g strong wholemeal flour
25g strong white flour
25g rolled oats
1 tablespoon vinegar
  (I use organic cider vinegar)
150ml water
2 tablespoons extra virgin olive oil
25ml lukewarm water (see note)
1 tablespoon honey
10g fresh yeast, or 5g dried yeast
½ teaspoon salt

For the white bread
300g strong white flour
1 tablespoon vinegar
  (I use organic cider vinegar)
175ml water
1 tablespoon extra virgin olive oil
25ml lukewarm water (see note)
1 tablespoon honey
10g fresh yeast, or 5g dried yeast

Place the flour (and oats if making the wholemeal bread) in a bowl and add the vinegar, the larger amount of water and the olive oil. Mix to a dough, then cover the bowl with a clean tea towel and set aside in your kitchen for 24–48 hours.

▶

When you're ready to go to the next stage, place the 25ml of lukewarm water in a bowl or jug and stir in the honey (you can use molasses for the wholemeal bread if you prefer), then crumble in the yeast. Do not stir, but set aside for 5 minutes. Now place the dough in the bowl of a stand mixer with the dough hook attached and pour in the yeast mixture. Turn on the machine, just slowly at first, to mix the liquid into the dough. Once it's mixed in, add the salt and continue to knead for 7–10 minutes, scraping down the sides of the bowl after 5 minutes, until the dough is coming away from the sides of the bowl.

Drizzle a little olive oil over the dough and on the sides of the bowl and turn the dough upside down so that it's oiled underneath. Cover the bowl with a tea towel again and put it in a warm part of your kitchen until the dough has doubled in size. The white bread will be quite wet and the wholemeal bread slightly less wet. It may take anything between 1 and 2 hours to prove.

Once it's doubled in size, dip your finger in flour and gently press the top of the dough. If it springs back where you pressed it, it needs another bit of time to prove. If the dip from your finger stays indented, the dough is ready.

Knock the dough back with a lightly floured fist, then tip it into a 2lb loaf tin brushed with olive oil. I sometimes find that if the top of the loaf is looking a bit messy, it helps to turn it over to find the smoother side.

Dust flour over the top of the dough and place somewhere warm, covered with the tea towel once more, to have its final rise until doubled in size and not springing back when you press it with your finger. This may take 20–30 minutes, depending on the heat in your kitchen. Preheat the oven to 220°C/200°C fan/gas 7.

When the dough has finished rising, place the bread in the preheated oven, turning the temperature down to 200°C/180°C fan/gas 6 after 10 minutes. Continue to bake the bread for another 30–40 minutes, until it sounds hollow when you tap it on its base. I like to take the bread out of the tin 5–10 minutes before the end of baking, and put it back into the oven until it's ready. This gives a lovely crust all over.

When the bread is baked, take it out of the oven and cool on a wire rack.

 note *It's important not to have the water too hot when making yeast bread. Yeast is killed at anything above 55°C, but a nice lukewarm (body heat, 36°C) temperature works well – the dough will rise in the bowl a bit faster than using cold water, but it's not so hot that it'll kill it. If, however, you are proving the dough in the fridge overnight or for a long time during the day, you can just use cold water.*

Ballymaloe simple white yeast bread

Super-simple and speedy to make, this yeasted bread requires no kneading and only one rising, so it is a brilliant introduction to using yeast, or for when you want a delicious yeast-leavened bread that's ready quickly. Made from start to finish in about an hour and a half, it's perfect with soup or for toast or sandwiches.

450g strong white flour
1 teaspoon salt
1 teaspoon honey

300ml lukewarm water
  (see note, page 214)
20g fresh yeast, or 10g dried yeast
sesame or poppy seeds (optional)

In a wide mixing bowl, mix the flour with the salt and make a well in the centre.

In a small bowl or jug, mix the honey with the water, then crumble in the yeast. Set this aside for a few minutes to allow the yeast to start to work. After about 3–4 minutes the water will have a creamy and perhaps slightly frothy appearance on top. When it's ready, stir it, then pour it into the flour to make a loose dough. The mixture should be just too wet to knead.

Meanwhile, brush the base and sides of a 2lb loaf tin with olive oil. Scoop the dough mixture into the greased tin and smooth the top. Sprinkle the top of the loaf with sesame or poppy seeds if you wish.

Cover the loaf loosely with a clean tea towel and place in a warm part of your kitchen, somewhere close to the cooker, in a sunny window or near a radiator perhaps – this is not essential if there isn't a warm part of your kitchen – it will just take slightly longer if your kitchen is quite cool.

Preheat the oven to 230°C/210°C fan/gas 8. When the dough rises just over the top of the tin, after about 30 minutes (this varies depending on room temperature), remove the cloth and pop the loaf into the preheated oven.

After 20 minutes, turn the oven down to 200°C /180°C fan/gas 6 and bake the loaf for another 40 minutes, or until it is golden on top. Now take the bread out of the tin and tap its base. If it sounds hollow when tapped, it is cooked; if not, pop it back into the oven without the tin for another 5–10 minutes until baked. Cool on a wire rack.

White yeast bread and variations

This bread can be baked in loaf tins or made into plaits or rolls. This recipe makes 1.15kg of dough, so you can make 23 x 50g rolls, 2 x 1lb loaves, 1 large or 2 medium-sized plaits, or a combination.

400ml lukewarm water
  (see note, page 214)

2 teaspoons caster sugar

20g fresh yeast (or 10g dried yeast)

700g strong white flour (also called
  bread flour or bakers' flour)

2 teaspoons salt

25g butter

Place the lukewarm water in a jug and stir in the sugar, then take the spoon out and crumble in the yeast. Do not stir, and allow to stand for 3 minutes until it becomes slightly frothy or fizzy.

Meanwhile, place the flour in a wide mixing bowl or the bowl of a stand mixer, mix in the salt, then rub in the butter until it resembles coarse breadcrumbs.

Make a well in the centre of the flour and add the liquid, getting every bit of yeast out of the jug into the bowl. Mix to a dough, using the dough hook on the stand mixer, or with your hand or a wooden spoon. Cover with a tea towel and allow to rest for 5 minutes.

Uncover the dough and knead, either using the dough hook, or on the work surface by hand until silky and smooth – 5–6 minutes if using the machine, or 10 minutes approximately by hand. If using the machine, the dough will be coming away from the sides of the bowl when it's ready. To make sure it's been kneaded enough, press a floured finger into the dough and if it is springy, it's ready. Place the dough in a large mixing bowl if you've been kneading it by hand, or leave it in the food mixer bowl if that's what you've been using, and cover the bowl with a tea towel. Place in a warm part of your kitchen and leave to rise until at least doubled in size. It should just be on a sunny windowsill or somewhere warm, but again, not above 45°C. The dough will look very light when it's ready, and there should be no spring in it when you press it with a floured finger. This can take 1–2 hours. If you wish, you can place it, covered, in the fridge to rise very slowly for approximately 8 hours or overnight.

Meanwhile, preheat the oven to 230°C/210°C fan/gas 8. Knock back the dough by punching it a couple of times, then tip it out on to your work surface and knead for just 2 minutes. Cover with a tea towel and allow to rest for 5 minutes, then shape the dough into loaves, as follows, or however you wish (see variations below and on pages 219–221).

For the loaves, brush two 1lb loaf tins with olive oil. Divide the dough in half, fold over and shape the dough into a roll on a clean, un-floured work surface, and place, with the crease facing down, in the oiled tin. Repeat with the second loaf, then cover with a tea towel and allow to rise, somewhere nice and warm again, until doubled in size, which can take anywhere from 20 to 40 minutes depending on the yeast and the warmth of the water and the room. When you gently press the dough with a floured finger it shouldn't be so springy any more, just nice and light.

Spray with a water mister and dust with flour for a rustic-looking loaf and slash with a small sharp knife or blade if you want to create a design on top. You can also brush the top with egg wash (some beaten egg with a small splash of milk or cream) and sprinkle it with seeds.

The bread will rise a little further when it goes into the oven – this is called the oven-spring. Bake for 25–35 minutes, depending on size. If the bread has developed enough colour in the first 15 minutes, turn the oven down to 200°C/180°C fan/gas 6 and continue to cook until it is fully baked. When baked, the bread should sound hollow if tapped underneath once tipped out of the tins. Leave the baked bread to cool on a wire rack.

For the plait, take the white yeast dough after it has been knocked back and divide it into 3 equal pieces. Use both hands to roll each one into a salami-shaped piece, just on a clean work surface with no flour dusted over – the thickness depends on how fat you want the plait to be. It will shrink at first, so re-roll each piece a second time. Pinch the three ends together at the top, then bring each outside strand into the centre alternately to form a plait. Pinch the ends and tuck in neatly, then transfer to a baking tray and leave, covered with a tea towel, to double in size.

Bake at 230°C/210°C fan/gas 8 for 10 minutes, then reduce the temperature to 200°C/180°C fan/gas 6 and cook for another 20–30 minutes, until the plait sounds hollow when you tap it on its base.

Bread – soup broth bread

Bread rolls

Divide the dough into 30g or 50g pieces, depending on the size of rolls you want. Shape on a clean un-floured work surface, with the palm of your hand cupped over the top of the dough and moving clockwise or anti-clockwise to form a roll. You can make a roll with each hand at the same time if you wish. Always remember to keep any dough covered with a tea towel or upturned bowl while you're not using it. Transfer the rolls, smooth side up, to a floured baking tray and cover with a tea towel until doubled in size.

Bake in the preheated oven (230°C/210°C fan/gas 8) for 10–20 minutes, depending on the size, and your oven.

Garlic butter knots

Cut the dough into 30g or 50g pieces, depending on the size of knots you want. Roll each piece on an un-floured work surface, always remembering to keep the rest of the dough covered with a tea towel or upturned bowl, into a length like a salami, either 30cm long for the 50g piece of dough, or 23cm long for the 30g piece. Then form into a knot and place on a floured baking tray, leaving a little space between them as they'll double in size. Cover with a tea towel and leave to rise until doubled in size, then bake for 8–14 minutes.

While the knots are baking, or proving, make the garlic butter – either way, have it ready and hot for when the knots come out of the oven.

Garlic butter

Enough for 15 knots

50g butter
2 large cloves of garlic, crushed or finely grated
2 teaspoons chopped parsley

Place the butter in a small saucepan with the garlic over a medium heat and allow to melt. Cook for another half minute or so, until the butter is foaming, then add the chopped parsley and take off the heat. When the baked knots come out of the oven, immediately brush them generously with the garlic butter and allow to cool slightly before eating.

Anchoïade

2 cloves of garlic, finely grated or crushed
1 tin of anchovies, drained and mashed
1 egg yolk
juice of ½ a lemon
200ml extra virgin olive oil
salt and freshly ground pepper

Put the garlic, anchovies, egg yolk and lemon juice into a bowl or a food processor, and mix well. Add the oil gradually in a thin, steady stream while whisking all the time, or blend in the food processor. Season to taste.

Cheesy tear-and-share swirls

This can be baked in a 20cm high-sided round cake tin, or the slices can be baked on a baking tray so that they stay separate.

Serves 10

300g white yeast bread dough

100g grated cheese, such as Cheddar, Gruyère or similar

If baking this in a cake tin, brush the sides with olive oil and line the base with a disc of parchment paper. Otherwise, dust a baking tray with flour. Roll the knocked-back dough into a 20 x 30cm rectangle, then scatter the cheese all over, leaving a 2cm empty margin down the two long sides. Brush one of the margins with a little water, then, starting from the other long side, roll it into a long roll and finally use the wet edge to stick it in place.

Place the dough seam-side down, and cut it into 10 even slices, each 3cm thick. Lay the slices flat and neaten them into rounds again, just in case they've been slightly squashed. Place them in the tin (3 in the centre and 7 around the sides, just touching each other), or sit them separately on the baking tray. Cover with a tea towel and leave until light and doubled in size.

Bake at 230°C/210°C fan/gas 8 for 10 minutes, then turn the oven down to 200°C/180°C fan/ gas 6 and bake for another 20–25 minutes, until golden and cooked through. If they're on a baking tray, they'll only take 10 minutes at 230°C/210°C fan/gas 8, then another 5–7 minutes at 200°C/180°C fan/gas 6.

Remove from the baking tray or tin, peel off any paper, and make sure they're baked underneath. These are best eaten warm.

note

For some extra indulgence you can brush melted garlic butter (see page 219) over these when they come out of the oven.

Black olive, thyme and cheese swirls

Makes 10

300g dough

50g chopped olives

2 generous teaspoons chopped thyme (rosemary can also be used)

75g grated cheese, such as Parmesan

Follow the previous recipe, but using the olives, thyme and Parmesan to fill the roll instead. Roll, cut and bake as described. Or you can knead the filling mixture directly into the dough to make black olive, thyme and cheese bread rolls.

Fougasse (VG)

I love these Provençal flatbreads, which are not completely dissimilar to Italian focaccia. Use extra virgin olive oil and lots of rosemary and thyme for the best result. These are great served with a bowl of anchoïade, and sometimes I like to spread the anchoïade over the top of the dough before baking, which cooks the anchovies in the Provençal mayonnaise, giving you a different flavour.

For each large fougasse you will need:

300g white yeast bread dough
2–3 tablespoons extra virgin olive oil
1 teaspoon chopped mixed rosemary and thyme
sea salt flakes

Line a baking tray with parchment paper, then roll the dough out on the work surface until it is about 5mm thick, in a large leaf shape. Lift it on to the baking tray and use your fingertips to stretch it out a little bit more. Use a sharp knife or a blade to cut slits in the dough to resemble the veins on a leaf, with one long slit down the centre and two or three on either side of the leaf at an angle. Don't cut through the paper if possible. Gently pull the dough so that the cut veins stay wide open and don't join together again. Cover the dough with a tea towel and let it sit for about 20 minutes, until puffy, and almost twice the thickness.

Preheat the oven to 230°C/210°C fan/gas 8. Just before putting the fougasse into the preheated oven to bake, gently brush the surface with olive oil and scatter with the chopped herbs. Sprinkle sea salt over the top and bake for 15–20 minutes, until golden brown. Cool slightly, then serve.

Focaccia-style soda bread

Inspired by the classic Italian focaccia, this is a delicious bread that's made in minutes and is great served with a big bowl of soup. I always use extra virgin olive oil for the best result. Do ensure that the dough is not too dry or overhandled, otherwise the bread will be heavy.

Before it goes into the oven, feel free to add extra ingredients on top of the dough: wedges of red onion, olives, roasted peppers, grilled aubergine slices or cheese.

50ml extra virgin olive oil
450g plain flour
1 teaspoon salt
½ teaspoon bicarbonate of soda

400–425ml buttermilk
  (for a dairy-free option, see note)
a few sprigs of rosemary, broken
  into small pieces
sea salt flakes
25ml extra virgin olive oil, for the top

Preheat the oven to 230°C/210°C fan/gas 8. Brush the inside of a small Swiss roll tin generously with some of the olive oil.

Sift the flour, salt and bicarbonate of soda into a large wide mixing bowl and make a well in the centre.

Pour most of the buttermilk in at once, leaving just a couple of tablespoonfuls behind. Using one hand, shaped like a claw, start in the well of buttermilk in the centre and go in circles, clockwise or anti-clockwise, to gradually mix in the flour from the sides of the bowl, adding the last bit of buttermilk if necessary. The dough should be soft, and a bit wet and sticky.

When it all comes together, turn the dough out on to a floured work surface (I usually wash the dough off my hands at this stage), then turn it over in the flour once (but making sure not to knead it in any way, or you will make it tough), and gently roll it out so that it will fit into the Swiss roll tin.

Transfer the dough to the tin using both hands. Drizzle the remaining olive oil over the top, making dimples with the tips of your fingers, to make little wells for the olive oil to sit in. Sprinkle with the rosemary tufts (pressing them gently into the dough so that they don't fall off when the bread is baked) and scatter over the sea salt.

Bake in the preheated oven for about 25–30 minutes, or until cooked. When it's ready, the bread should be nice and golden on top and on the bottom.

If the bread gets a good golden colour and you don't want it to darken any more while cooking, turn the oven down to 200°C/180°C fan/gas 6 and continue cooking.

As soon as the focaccia is cooked, drizzle a little more olive oil over the top to make it glisten – this will soak into the bread, leaving a delicious flavour and texture. Allow to cool slightly before serving.

 note *For a dairy-free version, use a plant-based drink such as almond drink or oat drink, with the addition of 1 tablespoon of vinegar or 2 tablespoons of lemon juice.*

Brown soda bread

Makes a 2lb loaf

There's something supremely comforting about the aroma of a freshly baked loaf of soda bread. A simple loaf, this can be hard to beat when it's enjoyed still warm, with butter melting into each slice.

225g wholemeal flour, coarse if possible
225g plain flour
1 scant teaspoon bicarbonate of soda
1 generous teaspoon salt

15g butter
1 egg
375–400ml buttermilk

Preheat the oven to 220°C/200°C fan/gas 7.

Place the wholemeal flour in a large wide mixing bowl, then sift in the plain flour and the bicarbonate of soda, and add the salt. Add the butter and rub into the flour mixture with your fingertips until it resembles coarse breadcrumbs. Make a well in the centre.

In another bowl, whisk the egg with the buttermilk, then pour most of the liquid (all but 3 tablespoons) into the well in the centre of the flour. Using one hand, with your fingers outstretched like a claw, bring the flour and liquid together, moving your claw-like hand around in circles, adding more buttermilk if, when the dough starts to come together, there are dry bits in the bottom of the bowl. The dough should be quite soft, but not too sticky. Do not knead the mixture. Firm but quick handling is the key here.

Turn on to a floured work surface. I find it useful to wash my hands at this stage. Then, with clean floured hands, gently bring the dough together into a round cake, about 4–5cm deep/thick, turning it over once, as the underside is often better-looking than the top side. Transfer the loaf to a slightly floured baking tray, then, using a sharp knife with a sawing motion, cut a cross on top, going down about 1cm into the dough.

Place in the preheated oven and bake for 15 minutes, then turn down the heat to 200°C/180°C fan/gas 6 and cook for 25–30 minutes more. When cooked, the loaf will sound hollow when tapped on the base. Allow to cool on a wire rack. If you want a softer crust, wrap the bread in a clean tea towel as soon as it comes out if the oven, until cool.

note *To make this dairy-free, swap the buttermilk for a plant-based drink with 1 tablespoon of vinegar added. Omit the butter, or use coconut oil instead to give a soft tender crumb. The egg can be omitted, but you'll need a little extra buttermilk instead.*

Debbie's gluten-free white soda bread

Makes 2x 1lb loaves

This recipe was kindly given to me by Debbie Shaw, who teaches with me at the Ballymaloe Cookery School. Debbie is a nutritionist and all-round super-hero when it comes to creating delicious recipes for various food intolerances!

450g Bob's Red Mill all purpose gluten-free flour or Doves Farm gluten-free plain white flour

1 level teaspoon salt

1 level teaspoon bicarbonate of soda, finely sieved

scant ½ teaspoon xanthan gum

1 teaspoon gluten-free baking powder

1 tablespoon ground mixed seeds, such as flax, pumpkin and sunflower seeds

1 egg, whisked

1 tablespoon olive oil

350–400ml sour milk or buttermilk

1 tablespoon whole mixed seed, for the top (optional)

First, fully preheat your oven to 230°C /210°C fan/gas 8. Line two 1lb loaf tins with parchment paper.

Sift the dry ingredients into a wide bowl and add the ground seeds. Make a well in the centre and add the whisked egg and olive oil. Pour most of the milk in at once. Using one hand, mix in the flour from the sides of the bowl, adding more milk if necessary. The dough should be soft, and a bit wet. When it all comes together (do not overmix), pour into the lined tins. Sprinkle the top with seeds if using.

Bake for 15 minutes, then turn down the oven to 200°C/180°C fan/gas 6 and bake for 20 minutes, or until cooked. If you are in doubt, tap the bottom of the bread: if it is cooked it will sound hollow and should feel light.

Take the bread out of the tin and bake for 5–8 minutes more to get a lovely crunchy crust.

Ballymaloe Cookery School focaccia

This is the focaccia that we make at the Ballymaloe Cookery School, a recipe devised and tweaked over time by my father-in-law, Tim.

The secret of a super-light Italian focaccia is to incorporate enough water into the dough, which is why it is added in increments in this recipe, allowing for the gluten in the flour to be developed before more water is added. We always teach our students to weigh the water for this recipe to get exact measurements, because if a little bit too much liquid goes in with each addition of water, the dough will just end up too wet.

This particular recipe works best using a stand mixer and dough hook – however, if you don't have one, you can make it by hand but it'll take some time and patience to get it to the right stage. The original Italian bread was simply sprinkled with flakes of sea salt, but we often add a couple of teaspoons of chopped rosemary, thyme or sage over the top of the focaccia with the sea salt flakes before baking, and, if you wish, about 15 pitted olives can also be added, though it's worth pressing them down into the dough so they stick.

Sometimes when a freshly baked focaccia is taken from the oven, it gets drizzled with another glug of extra virgin olive oil. I feel it's not necessary with this recipe, but do so if the mood takes you.

600g lukewarm water (see above, and note on page 214)

15g caster sugar

20g fresh yeast, or 10g dried yeast

2 tablespoons extra virgin olive oil, plus extra for drizzling into the bowl and the tray

700g strong white flour

2 teaspoons salt

sea salt flakes

Place 150g of the lukewarm water in a bowl or measuring jug and stir in the caster sugar. Add the yeast and set aside for 3 minutes. Add the olive oil and another 300g of lukewarm water.

Place the flour and salt in the bowl of a stand mixer fitted with the dough hook, and mix together. Make a well in the centre and pour in the yeast mixture. Mix to a dough – this will take approximately 5 minutes.

▸

Add half the remaining lukewarm water (75g) and continue to knead, using the dough hook, for another 5–6 minutes until it comes together again, then add the remainder of the lukewarm water (75g). Continue to knead for another 6–10 minutes until the dough becomes soft, silky and stretchy – it should now be coming away from the sides of the bowl.

Pour the dough out on to a clean, damp work surface for 'bench rest'. Gently fold the dough from each side into the centre like a parcel. Rest for 5 minutes. Repeat twice more, resting for 5 minutes each time. After you have folded the dough the third time, transfer it to a bowl oiled with olive oil (you can use the bowl of the stand mixer again). Cover the bowl with a clean tea towel, set aside in a slightly warm part of your kitchen, and allow the dough to rise until about doubled in size, approximately 1–2 hours. The rising time will depend on the temperature of the water, the room and the freshness of the yeast being used. You can slow down this stage by placing the covered bowl in the fridge, where it'll take approximately 8–12 hours to rise. If I want to make the dough and bake the focaccia the following day, I will use all room temperature water instead of lukewarm water and place it in the fridge overnight.

Preheat the oven to 230°C/210°C fan/gas 8. You need a small deep roasting tin, measuring 32 x 23cm and 5cm deep. If you wish, you can line the tin with parchment paper – the base and up the sides too – just to ensure that the dough won't stick. Either way, brush the tin or the paper with olive oil.

When the dough has doubled in size, pour it from the oiled bowl into the oiled roasting tray, gently so as not to knock any air from the dough. Drizzle a little extra virgin olive oil over the top, and dimple the dough with your fingertips. Set aside somewhere nice and warm (but not above 40°C) for 15–20 minutes, to rise a bit more. Sprinkle with sea salt and cook in the preheated oven for 10–15 minutes, then reduce the temperature to 200°C/180°C fan/gas 6 and bake for a further 10–15 minutes. Remove from the tin and return to the oven, directly on the oven rack, for 5 minutes approximately, until light – it should sound hollow when tapped.

Cool on a wire rack.

Rye bread

This straightforward and quick-to-prepare rye bread is inspired by the brown yeast bread that we make at Ballymaloe, which in turn was based on the Grant loaf, created by baker Doris Grant during the Second World War to help people eat well on their rations, and unique in that it required no kneading and just one rise. This bread is quite light, due to the addition of wholemeal and white flour. Add a couple of tablespoons of sesame or caraway seeds to the mixture as well if you fancy.

1 generous teaspoon treacle or molasses

450ml lukewarm water (see note, page 214)

20g fresh yeast, or 7g dried yeast

150g wholemeal rye flour

150g strong wholemeal flour

100g strong white flour

1 teaspoon salt

caraway or sesame seeds (optional)

Stir the treacle or molasses into the lukewarm water, then crumble in the yeast but don't stir it in. Set aside for about 5 minutes, until the yeast starts to work. While you're waiting, place the rye flour, wholemeal flour and strong white flour in a large mixing bowl. Add the salt, and mix to combine. Make a well in the centre.

Check the yeast mixture – the surface will look a bit fizzy or frothy when it's ready. Stir well and pour all but 50ml of the liquid into the dry ingredients. Mix well to bring together – it should be soft and sloppy. If it's not, add the remaining water. Allow the mixture to stand in the mixing bowl for 5 minutes.

While the mixture is standing, brush the inside of a 2lb loaf tin with olive oil. Pour the wet dough into the tin, levelling the top, and sprinkle with caraway or sesame seeds if you wish. Lay a clean dry tea towel over the top, then set aside for about 15–25 minutes, until almost doubled in size – the mixture should reach the top of the tin. Preheat the oven to 220°C/200°C fan/gas 7 while the dough is rising.

When the dough has risen, carefully place it in the centre of the preheated oven and cook for 1 hour, turning the oven down to 200°C/180°C fan/gas 6 after 15 minutes. Five minutes before the end, take the loaf out of the oven, remove the tin, then put the bread back in the oven for 5 minutes to crisp up the sides. When the bread is cooked, take it out of the oven and cool on a rack.

Guinness bread

A delicious wholemeal bread that has a deep, dark flavour from the Guinness or Irish stout. This recipe uses a whole 500ml can of stout to make 2 loaves, but you can make just one loaf by halving the recipe. The bread will freeze well if frozen when fresh, and if you like you can cut the loaf into slices before freezing.

(V)

800g coarse wholemeal flour
100g plain flour
50g rolled oats
2 teaspoons salt
2 teaspoons bicarbonate of soda
2 eggs
500ml Guinness or Irish stout

200ml buttermilk
2 teaspoons brown sugar, treacle or molasses
50g butter, melted, or 50ml extra virgin olive oil
1 tablespoon sesame, poppy, pumpkin or sunflower seeds (optional)

Preheat the oven to 200°C/180°C fan/gas 6. Brush the inside of two 2lb loaf tins with some olive oil or melted butter and set aside.

Place the wholemeal flour, plain flour, oats and salt in a large, wide mixing bowl. Sift in the bicarbonate of soda and mix everything together. Make a well in the centre.

Whisk the eggs in a separate bowl, then add the Guinness, buttermilk, brown sugar (or treacle or molasses) and the butter or olive oil. Whisk to mix.

Pour the wet ingredients into the dry ones (making sure to scrape out the wet bowl), then, using one hand in a claw position, mix everything together until combined.

Tip the mixture into the loaf tins, then gently shake the tins and cut down the centre of the loaves with a knife – this helps to give an even rise in baking. Scatter with seeds if you wish, and bake in the preheated oven for 60–70 minutes, until the loaves sound hollow when gently tapped on the base. I like to remove them from their tins for the last 10 minutes or so of baking, to get a nice crust on the bottom.

Cool on a wire rack. If you want a softer crust, wrap the bread in a clean tea towel until cool, as soon as it comes out of the oven.

note   *To make this bread dairy-free, use a plant-based drink with 1 tablespoon of vinegar added instead of the buttermilk.*

Oat bread

Makes a 2lb loaf

This great bread is super-simple to make. The mixture before baking doesn't look quite right, as it's heavy and doughy, but in the oven a fabulous transformation happens and you end up with a gorgeously nutty and nutritious loaf. Sometimes I add a couple of tablespoons of seeds, such as sesame seeds, to the mix, with more scattered on top.

425g rolled oats (not jumbo or
    pinhead)
1 teaspoon salt
1 teaspoon bicarbonate of soda

1 egg
500g natural yoghurt
1 teaspoon honey or treacle
    (optional)

Preheat the oven to 200°C/180°C fan/gas 6, and line the base of a 2lb loaf tin with parchment paper.

Put the oats and salt into a large bowl, then sift in the bicarbonate of soda. Make a well in the centre.

Whisk the egg into the yoghurt with the honey or treacle, if using. Pour the yoghurt and egg mixture into the dry ingredients and mix well. The dough is meant to be dry and sticky at this stage, so don't worry.

Scoop the dough into the tin and bake for 50 minutes. Turn out of the loaf tin and bake for a further 10 minutes.

Cool on a wire rack.

note   *To make this bread gluten-free, buy gluten-free oats.*

Buckwheat and sesame seed loaf

Makes a 2lb loaf

Another bread made using the soaking method (see page 212 for more on the nutritional benefits of this technique), this time a gluten-free loaf using the super-nutritious buckwheat. This bread is also delicious toasted. Feel free to replace the sesame seeds with pumpkin, sunflower or poppy seeds, or to omit the seeds completely.

400g buckwheat flour
1 large egg
475ml buttermilk

1 teaspoon salt
1 scant teaspoon bicarbonate of soda
1 tablespoon sesame seeds

Place the buckwheat flour in a bowl. In a separate bowl, whisk the egg, then pour in 400ml of buttermilk and mix well. Pour the wet ingredients into the flour and mix well – it'll be a stiff dough. Cover with a clean tea towel and set aside (not in the fridge) in your kitchen overnight.

Next day, preheat the oven to 200°C/180°C fan/gas 6. Grease a 2lb loaf tin with olive oil. Place the remaining 75ml of buttermilk in a bowl and mix in the salt and the sifted bicarbonate of soda.

Make a well in the centre of the dough that's been sitting overnight, then pour in the mix of buttermilk, salt and bicarbonate of soda. Using your hand or a wooden spoon, mix well together until you have a sloppy mixture that's completely combined.

Scatter some of the sesame seeds on to the sides and base of the greased loaf tin, then tip the bread mixture into the tin. Smooth the top of the dough, then scatter more sesame seeds over the top and bake in the centre of the preheated oven for 1 hour. Remove from the oven and tip the loaf out of the tin, then replace it in the oven and bake for 5–10 minutes more, until the bread sounds hollow when you tap it on its base.

Cool on a wire rack.

Blue cheese and walnut bread

Makes 2x 1lb loaves or approximately 15 rolls

If you prefer you can leave out the blue cheese or replace it with raisins. Roasted chopped hazelnuts and dried cranberries make a lovely alternative to the walnuts and blue cheese

325g strong white flour
125g strong wholemeal flour
1 teaspoon salt
1 teaspoon honey or sugar
300ml lukewarm water (see note, page 214)

20g fresh yeast, or 10g dried yeast
5 tablespoons extra virgin olive oil
150g roughly chopped walnuts
200g blue cheese, broken into chunks

Place the strong white and strong wholemeal flours in a bowl and mix in the salt. Stir the sugar or honey, whichever you're using, into the water to dissolve, then scatter in the yeast but do not stir. Leave for 3–4 minutes in a warm place, until the yeast starts to fizz slightly. Stir in 3 tablespoons of the olive oil, then pour this mixture into the flour and mix to a pliable dough.

Knead for about 10 minutes, preferably adding no flour to the dough while you are kneading it. It will eventually become smooth and springy. You may need to scrape the scraggly bits of dough from the work surface and your hands and work them into the ball of dough to help bring it together. Alternatively, knead the dough using a stand mixer and the dough hook. It will probably take just 6–8 minutes if using a mixer.

Put 1 tablespoon of olive oil into a clean bowl (it can be the same mixing bowl that you used to make the dough) and turn the dough in it to cover the surface and prevent a dry crust forming. Cover the bowl with a clean tea towel and leave the dough to rise in a warm place for about 1½–2 hours, or until it doubles in size. Knock back the dough by kneading it for 3 minutes, then divide it in half. Set one half aside while you work with the other and stretch it out into an oval, approximately 25cm in length. Scatter over half the chopped walnuts and chunks of blue cheese, then press them into the dough and roll the dough away from you, tucking it in well at the end. Turn it over so that the smooth side is facing up and repeat with the second piece of dough. Place the loaves on a baking tray brushed with a little olive oil or into oiled 1lb loaf

▶

tins. Cover them with a tea towel and let them rise again for about 45 minutes to 1 hour, or until doubled in size again.

Preheat the oven to 230°C/210°C fan/gas 8.

Brush the loaves with water to soften the crust and bake for about 40–45 minutes, turning the temperature down to 200°C/180°C fan/gas 6 after 10 minutes, or until they sound hollow when tapped on the bottom (cooking time depends on the size of the loaves). Brush with the remaining olive oil and cool on a wire rack.

You can also make blue cheese and walnut rolls by cutting the knocked-back dough into 50g pieces. Place one piece of dough on the work surface, covering the others with a tea towel, then, using your fingertips, spread out the small piece of dough and scatter over some of the blue cheese and walnuts. Now bring the edges all the way round into the centre, tucking them in, then turn the dough over so that the smooth side is on top. Using your hand cupped over the piece of dough, on a clean un-floured work surface, rotate your hand so that a smooth round roll forms underneath. Place on an oiled baking tray and repeat with the others.

The rolls can be baked at 230°C/210°C fan/gas 8 like the loaves of bread, but don't turn the oven down after 10 minutes. Continue to cook them at the higher temperature – they'll take about 10–15 minutes.

Buckwheat scones

Makes 8

Often hailed as a superfood, buckwheat is a highly nutritious ingredient that has been applauded for its many health benefits. It's not related to wheat, it's gluten-free and it's a great source of protein, energy and fibre. Thank you to my sister-in-law Emily for sharing her recipe with me.

(V)

(GF)

225g buckwheat flour

½ teaspoon salt

½ teaspoon bicarbonate of soda, sifted

1 egg

150ml buttermilk

Preheat the oven to 200°C/180°C fan/gas 6.

Place the buckwheat flour in a mixing bowl with the salt and the sifted bicarbonate of soda. Mix the dry ingredients with your hand and make a well in the centre.

In a separate bowl, whisk the egg, then add to the buttermilk and mix together. Pour all but 2 tablespoons of the mixture into the centre of the dry ingredients, then, with your hand shaped like a claw, move it in circles through the ingredients until they come together. Add the final 2 tablespoons of the liquid if it's too dry to come together.

Dust your work surface with a little buckwheat flour, then tip the dough out on to it. Wash your hands, then dust them with some flour and also dust the top of the dough. Tuck the dough in at the edges, then gently turn it over so that the smoother side is on top. Pat the dough out with the palm of your hand until it is 2cm thick, then cut into 8 scones and place on a baking tray dusted with a little buckwheat flour.

Bake the scones in the oven for just 13 minutes, until they're golden brown underneath. They will be cracked on top but still pale. Take one scone out, tap it on its base, and if it sounds hollow, they are baked. Place on a rack to cool.

note   *If you like, you can scatter sesame or pumpkin seeds over the top of the scones. Just brush any remaining buttermilk and egg, or just some extra buttermilk, over them before they go into the oven, then scatter with seeds and bake as above.*

Pumpkin, cheese and rosemary scones

Makes 9

Deliciously savoury and gorgeously light in texture, these scones are great served with a big bowl of soup. You can use any squash instead of pumpkin, and, if you fancy, add lardons of crispy bacon or diced chorizo to the mix.

175g peeled and deseeded pumpkin (weight when peeled and deseeded)

1 tablespoon olive oil

200g plain flour

1½ teaspoons baking powder

a pinch of cayenne pepper

2 teaspoons finely chopped rosemary

½ teaspoon salt

50g finely grated cheese (Cheddar or a hard cheese such as Parmesan)

1 egg

100ml milk, plus 1 tablespoon extra for brushing the top

Preheat the oven to 200°C/180°C fan/gas 6.

Cut the pumpkin into 1–2cm chunks and place on a roasting tray. Drizzle with the olive oil and roast in the oven for about 20 minutes, until completely tender. Tip the pumpkin into a bowl (leaving the oven on) and mash very well with a fork, or blend in a food processor, then allow to cool. If using canned pumpkin purée, you'll need 125g.

Sift the flour, baking powder and cayenne into a bowl and add in the rosemary, salt and all but 2 tablespoons of the grated cheese, reserving the remaining cheese for scattering over the scones before they go into the oven.

Whisk the egg and mix with the pumpkin purée and milk. Make a well in the centre of the dry ingredients and add the wet ingredients, then, with your hand in a claw shape, mix the two, making sure you don't knead but just mixing until it comes together.

Tip the mixture out on to a floured surface and tidy the sides, working it into a rough square and patting the dough out to 2cm thick. Brush a little milk over the top and scatter with the remaining cheese, then cut the dough into 3 x 3, to make 9 scones.

Place the scones on a baking tray and bake in the preheated oven for about 15 minutes, or until golden and cooked through. They should sound hollow when tapped on the base. Cool on a wire rack.

Debbie's gluten-free chorizo and Cheddar scones

Makes 6–8

Here's another great gluten-free bread recipe from my fellow Ballymaloe Cookery School teacher and nutritionist friend, Debbie Shaw. These completely delicious scones are perfect enjoyed with a big hearty bowl of soup.

Make sure that the chorizo that you are using is gluten-free – Debbie uses our local chorizo, made in West Cork by our friend Fingal Ferguson.

350g Bob's Red Mill all purpose gluten-free flour (or your favourite plain gluten-free flour), sieved, plus a little extra for shaping the dough

½ teaspoon bicarbonate of soda

1 rounded teaspoon gluten-free baking powder

scant ½ teaspoon salt

110g mature Cheddar cheese, grated

50g gluten-free chorizo, very finely diced

1 large egg, whisked

175–235ml buttermilk or natural yoghurt

1 teaspoon olive oil

Preheat the oven to 230°C/210°C fan/gas 8.

Place the flour, bicarbonate of soda, baking powder and salt in a wide bowl and mix well. Add most of the cheese (reserving 4 tablespoons for the top of the scones) and the diced chorizo and mix well. Now add half the egg, the buttermilk and the olive oil, and mix gently to form a soft dough. If it is a bit wet, add a little more flour. Turn the dough out on to a well-floured surface, shape into a rectangle 4cm thick, and cut into 6–8 scones, depending on how big you want them.

Place on a lightly floured tray and bake in the preheated oven for 15–20 minutes, until golden and light. Pop the scones on a cooling rack for a few minutes.

These yummy scones are best enjoyed on the day that they're baked, warm from the oven.

Cheesy muffins

Makes 12

These simple and delicious cheesy muffins are great on a cold, blustery day with a big bowl of soup. They transport well for a packed lunch and are a lovely addition to a picnic.

This basic recipe can be tweaked and changed to suit your taste. Add chopped chives, bacon, chorizo, olives or halved cherry tomatoes if you like. Sometimes I add a teaspoon of smoked paprika in place of the cayenne. If using chorizo or bacon, dice it finely and cook it before adding it to the muffin mix.

75g butter
250g plain flour
2 teaspoons baking powder
½ teaspoon salt
½ teaspoon cayenne pepper

125g grated cheese (use a mixture of Cheddar, Gruyère and Parmesan, or just Cheddar)
1 large egg
250ml milk
1 generous teaspoon Dijon mustard

Preheat the oven to 190°C/170°C fan/gas 5. Line a 12-cup muffin tray with paper cases.

Melt the butter and set aside. Sift the flour and baking powder into a bowl. Add the salt and cayenne, then mix in the grated cheese.

Whisk the egg in a separate bowl and stir in the melted butter, the milk and the Dijon mustard. Make a well in the centre of the dry ingredients and stir in the wet ingredients until combined.

Divide the mixture among the paper cases and bake in the oven for approximately 20 minutes, or until golden and a skewer will come out clean from the centre of a muffin.

To make cheese and chorizo (or bacon) muffins, cut 150g of chorizo (or bacon) into fine dice, then cook in a frying pan with 1 tablespoon of olive oil over a low heat for 4–5 minutes, until just golden and the fats have rendered out. Drain on kitchen paper. Add to the muffin mix with the egg and butter.

Brazilian cheese bread

Makes 8

Pao de queijo, or Brazilian cheese bread, had up until recently completely escaped my knowledge, until restaurateur Nicola Zammit from Two Cooks in Kildare told me about it.

It can be made in a few different ways: sometimes it contains mashed potato, at other times it's blended together, or, like this version, it's made in a similar way to a choux pastry and cooked in a pan before it's baked.

More like cheese puffs than an actual bread, tapioca flour is used in every version I've seen, instead of wheat flour, making this gluten-free. And like choux pastry cheese puffs, or gougères, little cubes of chorizo or cooked crispy bacon work a treat in these too. Delicious eaten while still a little warm, this bread can also be reheated.

50ml extra virgin olive oil
75ml milk
75ml water
½ teaspoon salt

115g tapioca flour
1 egg
50g grated Parmesan or Grana Padano
a pinch of cayenne pepper

Preheat the oven to 200°C/180°C fan/gas 6. Place the olive oil in a saucepan with the milk and the water over a high heat. Bring to the boil, then take off the heat and immediately add the salt and the tapioca. Using a wooden spoon (not a whisk, as the mixture will get too thick), bring the mixture together. It'll look a bit uneven, but don't worry, that's fine. Set the mixture in the saucepan aside while you whisk the egg in a bowl.

Now, stir in the egg, grated cheese and cayenne (and 75g of finely diced chorizo or sautéd crispy bacon, if you like).

Using 2 dessertspoons, or something similar, take a heaped spoonful of the mixture, and with the other spoon, scoop it off the first spoon on to a baking tray so that it resembles a scoop of ice cream or mashed potato. There's no need to grease or line the baking tray. Repeat until the mixture is all finished – you should get about 8 from this quantity.

Place in the preheated oven and bake for 20–22 minutes, until golden brown all over. The mixture, containing no raising agent, can be made in advance and stored in the fridge for up to 48 hours if you wish.

Chilli cheese corn bread

Makes a 2lb loaf

Some breads are just ideal for serving with big meaty soups and stews. This bread, a Southern US classic, works really well with Mexican chilaquiles soup (see page 84), Santa Fe soup (see page 110) and the Mexican chicken broth (see page 33).

175g plain flour

175g medium maize meal (also called cornmeal or polenta)

50g caster sugar

2½ teaspoons baking powder

1 teaspoon salt

75g corn kernels (you can use frozen or tinned corn if fresh is unavailable)

50g grated Cheddar cheese

4 spring onions, trimmed and thinly sliced

2 tablespoons chopped coriander

½–1 red chilli

1 egg

50g butter, melted

225ml buttermilk

1 teaspoon Tabasco

Preheat the oven to 200°C/180°C fan/gas 6. Line the base and sides of a 10 x 20cm square tin with parchment paper.

Place the flour, maize meal, sugar, baking powder and salt in a mixing bowl, and mix together. Add the corn, grated cheese, sliced spring onions and chopped coriander. Cut the stalk end off the chilli and shake the seeds out, rolling the chilli in your hands to help them loosen (if you want very spicy corn bread, keep the seeds in!). Now slice the chilli very finely and add to the bowl.

In a separate bowl, whisk the egg, then add the melted butter, buttermilk and Tabasco.

Make a well in the centre of the dry ingredients and add the wet ingredients, stirring to combine.

Tip the mixture into the prepared tin, then place in the centre of the oven and bake for approximately 30 minutes, or until golden brown and a skewer inserted into the centre comes out clean.

Lift the corn bread out of the tin and cool slightly, then cut into 6 rectangles or 9 squares, depending on how many you're serving. This is delicious spread with soft butter.

Japanese milk bread – shokupan

This quantity will make one 23cm tear-and-share loaf or fill two 1lb loaf tins

This is a Japanese tear-and-share loaf with the most wonderful pillowy soft texture. It's inspired by the Yudane and Tangzhong method, where a little bit of flour and water or milk (both, in this case) are cooked together to make a white sauce before mixing in the remaining ingredients. This method pre-gelatinizes the starch in the flour, allowing it to absorb more liquid and giving you a super-light bread that stays fresh for longer, as it retains its moisture.

I weigh all ingredients for this bread, including the liquid, as the measurements are very precise.

It also is divine with cinnamon, dried fruit and/or candied peel added as a sweet treat.

(V)

50g water (see above, and note, page 214)

50g milk

15g strong white flour

375g strong white flour

15g milk powder

25g caster sugar

1 teaspoon salt

115g milk

1 egg, beaten

25g fresh yeast, or 12g dried yeast

50g butter, melted

1 egg, whisked, for brushing the top

a pinch of salt

Pour the water and the milk into a small saucepan and bring to the boil. Add the 15g of flour and cook, whisking all the time, over the heat for a couple of minutes, until the liquid has thickened to a white sauce. Tip every bit out of the saucepan into a bowl and set aside to cool.

Place the 375g of strong white flour in a mixing bowl, or the bowl of a stand mixer with the dough hook attached, along with the milk powder, sugar and salt. Mix these ingredients so that the yeast doesn't go directly on to the salt, as this can kill the yeast.

Now place the milk (no need to heat it) in a separate bowl, or a jug, and add the beaten egg, the yeast and the melted butter. Stir, then pour all this liquid into the dry ingredients and mix to a dough. Knead the mixture for 8–10 minutes by hand, or about 5–6 minutes in the machine, until you have a smooth and almost springy dough – it's

►

not necessary to add flour while you're kneading, as the dough is supposed to be slightly sticky. If you're kneading by hand and the dough is sticking to your hands, just gather it up into a ball and clean the work surface with the help of a dough scraper or a palette knife, then flour your hands and continue to knead. When I'm using a stand mixer for this, I scrape down the sides of the bowl a couple of times during kneading.

When the dough has been kneaded enough, it will be smooth on the outside. Press it with a floured finger and the dent that you make should spring back a little bit.

Place the dough in a bowl large enough to take it when doubled in size (or leave it in the stand mixer bowl) and cover the bowl with a clean tea towel, clingfilm or a plate. Place it somewhere warm, not above 45°C, or just stand it on the counter in your kitchen and allow the dough to double in size (this may take 2 hours). If you wish, you can place the covered bowl of dough in the fridge overnight.

When the dough has doubled in size, punch the dough down to knock it back, using a floured fist, then knead it for just 1 minute.

Now, it's time to shape the dough into either a tear-and-share loaf or two 1lb loaves.

If you're making a tear-and-share loaf, brush the inside of a 23cm springform tin (you can also use a 25cm springform tin) with melted butter, then dust it with flour. Divide the dough into 8 equal pieces, each weighing about 90g. Keep all the dough covered with a clean tea towel while you work with one piece at a time. On a very lightly floured work surface, place one ball of dough. Fold the edges, all the way round, into the centre of the ball of dough, squashing it down in the centre as you go. Turn the ball over so that the folded side is on the underside and the smooth side is on top. Roll the ball gently under the palm of your hand to make a round roll, then place in the prepared tin. Repeat with all the other balls of dough, so that you end up with 7 around the sides, spaced apart, and one ball in the centre.

If you're making 2 loaves of bread, brush the inside of two 1lb loaf tins with melted butter and dust with flour. Divide the dough into 6 equal pieces, each weighing about 120g. Take one ball of dough, keeping the others covered with a tea towel, and on a very lightly floured work surface, fold in the edges, all the way round, into the centre of the ball of dough, squashing it down in the centre as you go, then roll the ball of dough, with a light dusting of flour to stop it sticking, into an oval about 20cm long. Fold in the left side and the right side (of the long sides) into the centre so that it looks like an envelope. Now roll, starting at one of the short ends, away from you, or towards you, to make a short roll. Place this smooth side up on the loaf tin, with the 'swirled' sides next to the long sides of the tin and repeat with 2 more, placing them next to each other. Repeat with the remaining 3 pieces of dough to make the second loaf.

Now cover with the tea towel again and place on the work surface or somewhere a little warmer, again not above 45°C, and allow to rise again until almost doubled in size, about 35–45 minutes.

Preheat the oven to 200°C/180°C/gas 6. The dough is ready when you make a little dent with a floured finger and it doesn't spring back. Also, the balls of dough should have joined together at this stage. Whisk the egg with a pinch of salt and brush very gently over the top of the risen bread. Place the bread in the lower part of the preheated oven to bake for 30-40 minutes. The dough, out of the tin, should sound hollow when you tap it on the base. If you wish, you can bake the bread out of the tin for the last 5 minutes of the cooking time. Place on a wire rack to cool.

Pitta bread

Making your own pitta bread is really satisfying. Light, puffy rounds, or ovals, of yeast-leavened bread, just perfect for serving with soup or indeed filling with whatever you fancy.

If you want to give your pittas an extra bit of flavour, roll each ball of dough in 1 teaspoon of sesame seeds, cumin seeds or chopped rosemary before rolling into rounds or ovals.

Any leftover pittas can be cut into wedges and made into toasted pitta wedges (see page 190).

325ml lukewarm water (see note, page 214)

1 teaspoon sugar

25g fresh yeast, or 12g dried yeast

450g strong white flour

1 teaspoon salt

Place the water in a measuring jug and stir in the sugar. Crumble in the yeast and set aside for 5 minutes.

Sift the flour into a bowl, add the salt and mix. Pour in the yeast mixture and mix well until combined. Turn out on to a work surface and knead the dough until it is very smooth – no need to add any extra flour – for about 8–10 minutes. The dough should be smooth on the outside and feel slightly springy to the touch. You can knead by hand or you can use a stand mixer with a dough hook, which will take about 5 minutes.

Once the dough is kneaded, rub a little olive oil around the inside of a mixing bowl (or the stand mixer bowl) and turn the dough so that the whole surface is oiled. Cover with a clean tea towel or clingfilm and leave to rise in a nice warm part of your kitchen (not above 45°C) for about 1–2 hours, or until the dough has more than doubled in volume. The dough should be very light, with some bubbles appearing on the surface. When you gently press it with a floured finger, the dough should start to collapse.

Knock back the dough by punching it in, then take it out of the bowl and knead it again for just a couple of minutes. Roll into a thick log and divide it into 8–10 equal-sized pieces.

Place the first ball of dough on the work surface in front of you (keeping all the others covered with a tea towel), then fold the edges, all the way round the ball into the centre, and press down to secure it. This helps to incorporate some air into the pitta breads, giving that characteristic pocket once baked.

Now turn the ball of dough upside down, so that the folded pieces are facing down. Dust on top and underneath with some flour, and repeat with all the remaining balls of dough. Cover the balls of dough with a tea towel and allow to prove again for 30 minutes, until they have doubled in size.

Preheat the oven to 230°C/210°C fan/gas 8, and place a baking sheet in the oven to get hot.

Once the balls of dough have doubled in size, roll them into rounds, or ovals, about 5mm thick and 15cm across, keeping the rest covered with a clean tea towel while you work with each one. Place the rolled pittas on a floured surface, cover again, and leave to sit for just 5–10 minutes, until slightly puffy and light.

Bake 3 or 4 pittas at a time on the hot baking sheet for just 2–3 minutes, or until very light golden and puffed.

Remove from the oven and, if not using immediately, leave to cool, covered with tea towels, on wire racks.

Naan bread

Naan bread needs no introduction, but it's a lot easier to make than people think, and the beauty of baking your own is that you can get creative and make lots of variations from the one batch of dough. Naans have a lovely soft, tender crumb, from the milk and yoghurt added to the dough. They can be made in advance and reheated, and can also be frozen after baking or even before being cooked. I adore them with lashings of garlic butter brushed over while still hot from the oven, or with lots of fresh coriander or spices added.

For the basic naan bread

20g fresh yeast, or 10g dried yeast

200ml whole milk, lukewarm (see note)

500g strong white bread flour

1 teaspoon salt

2 teaspoons caster sugar

1 egg, beaten

125g natural yoghurt

1 tablespoon olive oil

Crumble the yeast into a small bowl and add a little of the warm milk. Stir until the yeast is dissolved.

Place the flour in the bowl of a stand mixer and add the salt and sugar. Make a well in the centre and add the yeast mixture, egg, yoghurt, olive oil and the remaining milk. Mix with a dough hook for about 10 minutes, until you have a soft, smooth dough.

Grease a large mixing bowl with a little oil. Transfer the dough into the bowl, turning it in the oil to coat. Cover with clingfilm and leave to rise in a warm place for about an hour, or until doubled in size. Towards the end of the proving time, preheat the oven to 220°C/200°C fan/gas 7 and turn on the grill to its highest setting. Put two baking trays into the oven to get them as hot as you can.

Once proved, follow one of the recipes, over the page:

▶

Coriander and garlic naans

60g butter, melted

2 cloves of garlic, crushed

3 tablespoons chopped coriander (leaves and fine stalks)

sea salt flakes

Combine the melted butter and garlic in a small bowl and set aside.

Roll the dough out on a floured surface. Sprinkle the coriander over half the dough and fold the other half over so that the coriander is sandwiched. Roll out again and fold to fully seal the herbs within the dough. Cut the dough into 6 pieces and cover them with clingfilm.

Roll out a piece of dough to about 3mm thick in a teardrop shape. Carefully but quickly, take one of the hot trays from the oven and transfer the dough to it. Put it back in the oven for about 5 minutes, until puffing up. Depending on your oven, it may be browned on top – if not, pop it under the grill for a few seconds to brown the top. Remove from the oven or grill and wrap it in a clean tea towel to keep warm while you make the others.

Repeat the process with the other 5 pieces of dough, alternating trays as you go so that one is always warming up again underneath.

Once they are all cooked, brush the naans with the garlic butter, sprinkle generously with sea salt flakes, and serve.

Spiced naans

1½ teaspoons nigella seeds

1½ teaspoons black mustard seeds

1½ teaspoons cumin seeds

sea salt flakes

60g butter, melted

Combine the nigella, black mustard and cumin seeds in a small bowl.

Cut the dough into 6 pieces and cover them with clingfilm. Take the first piece and roll it out to a teardrop shape about 3mm thick on a floured surface. Sprinkle it with about ½ teaspoon of the spice seed mix and a generous pinch of sea salt flakes. Roll gently over the top with the rolling pin to impress the spices into the dough.

Cook as for the coriander and garlic naan above. Once all the bread is cooked, brush it with plain melted butter and serve.

note

When heating the milk, ensure that it is just lukewarm. If it gets above 50°C, the yeast will be killed. See also note on page 214.

Bao buns

Also known as *baozi*, Chinese bao are soft and almost-fluffy yeast-leavened buns (*bao* means bun) that are generally cooked in a steamer. They're fun to make and are so divine when served with the sticky pork with sesame filling (see page 205) or with a bowl of egg drop soup (see page 54).

Traditionally sunflower or vegetable oil is used, but I prefer to use extra virgin olive oil instead.

The dough will freeze well at the point where the buns have been shaped but haven't had their final rising. Removed from the freezer, placed on the steamer and covered with a tea towel, they'll thaw and rise at the same time, taking around an extra hour or so.

50ml milk

15g caster sugar

8g fresh yeast, or 1 teaspoon dried yeast

250g plain flour

½ teaspoon salt

75g lukewarm water (see note, page 214)

1 tablespoon rice vinegar (or you can use Shaoxing rice wine, cider vinegar or white wine vinegar)

½ tablespoon olive oil

½ teaspoon baking powder

Warm the milk up to blood temperature (around 40°C, see note on page 256). Stir in the sugar and yeast, then set aside for 5 minutes to sponge the yeast.

Sift the flour and salt into a mixing bowl or the bowl of a stand mixer with the dough hook attached, and mix together.

Add the water, rice vinegar and olive oil to the milk and stir to mix, then pour into the flour. Mix until a dough is formed, then knead the dough for 8–10 minutes, until smooth and slightly springy. Cover the bowl with a tea towel and place in a warm part of your kitchen, not above 40°C, and allow to prove until doubled in size and very light and airy. When you press the surface with a floured finger, the light dough should start to fall back down. This may take 1½ –2 hours. You can also cover the bowl with clingfilm or a plate and leave it to prove overnight in the fridge, in which case just use cold water and milk, no need to heat it up.

▶

Knock back the dough when it's ready and while it's still in the bowl, sift over the baking powder. Knead the baking powder into the dough, then tip the dough out on to your work surface and knead for 2 minutes more. Leave to stand on the work surface, covered with a tea towel, for 5 minutes, to rest.

Cut a round of parchment paper that'll fit snugly inside your steamer. Fold it in half, then in half again, then in half again, so that you end up with a long triangle, and cut little nicks or triangles in the paper so that when you open it out, it looks a bit like a doily with lots of little holes in it. Alternatively, you can cut 8 squares of parchment paper, one for each individual bao bun to sit on. I normally just place them all on one piece.

Sit the parchment paper in the steamer. Don't place it over water on the heat yet.

Divide the dough into 8 even-sized balls, each one weighing approximately 50g, and while you work with one, keep the others covered with the tea towel. Place one ball of dough on the work surface and tuck the edges all the way round into the centre. Now turn the ball of dough over so that it's smooth on top, and roll into a circle with a 10cm diameter. The dough should be about 4mm thick all over. Brush the top surface of the round with olive oil, then fold in half – don't press down, you don't want to stick it together. Place on the paper and cover with a tea towel while you prepare the rest of the buns in the same way. Place them all on the paper in the steamer tray and cover with a tea towel. Place, again, in a warm part of your kitchen and let the buns sit for 1 hour, or until light and puffy.

When the buns are nearly ready, pour water into the base of your steamer and place it on a medium to high heat. Bring the water to the boil. When the buns are ready, lift the steamer tray and sit it over the water (not allowing it to touch the water), then cover with the lid and steam for 12 minutes, until cooked through. They won't have coloured on the outside but will be cooked in the centre.

Paratha

I have enjoyed paratha breads (sometimes called paranthe) in India, both fried and pan-cooked. In this recipe, I cook them in a small amount of ghee or butter in a pan and the flavour from the wholemeal flour sweetens and intensifies as the breads cook, darkening in spots in the fat . . . just delicious. Because they're rolled and brushed with fat, then folded and brushed, and folded and rolled again, you get lovely flaky layers in these delicious breads, which are great with the dal shorba on page 160 or the lentil soup with lemon and parsley on page 131.

If you ever happen to be in New Delhi, head to an area called Paranthe Wali Gali. It's a very narrow street with even more narrow streets jutting off it, famous for its fried parathas. The area is loud, hectic and bustling, a delightful onslaught on the senses, and the parathas are incredible. Sometimes, to bring me back to that magical place, I fry these paratha breads in a few centimetres of oil.

These can be dairy-free if you use oil instead of the butter or ghee. I prefer to use olive oil rather than a vegetable oil.

180g sifted wholemeal flour (weigh it after it has been sifted, then tip what's left in the sieve back into the bag of flour)

180g plain flour, plus extra for dusting
½ teaspoon salt
75g butter or ghee, melted
200ml water

Place the wholemeal flour, plain flour and salt in a bowl and mix together. Drizzle 2 tablespoons of the melted butter or ghee over the top and rub it in with your fingertips until the mixture resembles coarse breadcrumbs. Now add the water and bring the mixture together to form a ball of dough.

Tip the dough on to a clean work surface and knead it for about 8–10 minutes, or until you have a soft, springy dough that is smooth on the outside. Rub the dough all over with a small drizzle of the butter or ghee and place it on a plate, covered with an upturned bowl. Leave for 30 minutes or longer to rest.

Divide the dough into 16 equal-sized pieces and cover again with the upturned bowl. Take one piece of dough, keeping the remaining 15 covered, and place it on the work surface. Tuck the edges into the centre of the dough so that it forms a mini ball of dough, and turn it over so that the smooth side is facing you. Dust the work surface and the dough with plain flour and roll the dough into a circle approximately 15cm in diameter, dusting with a little more flour whenever necessary. Using a pastry brush, brush a little melted butter or ghee over half the surface of the circle of dough and fold it in half so that the buttered side is folded over the unbuttered side. Brush half the semicircle with melted butter or ghee, and again fold it in half to form a triangle. Roll out the triangle into a longer triangle that resembles a teardrop shape with sides measuring approximately 18cm, dusting with flour whenever necessary. Repeat with all the pieces of dough.

Place a large (and heavy, if possible) frying pan on a medium to low heat. Take a piece of kitchen paper and fold it into quarters. Now dab the kitchen paper into the melted butter or ghee and smear it over the base of the frying pan. Place two, if space allows, or otherwise just one paratha in the hot frying pan and cook for a minute. Brush the top of each paratha in the pan with the butter or ghee, then turn it over and cook on the second side for a minute or so. The parathas should not look raw and translucent but cooked and golden, and both sides should have dark brown spots.

Put the cooked paratha on a plate. Cover either with an upturned bowl or a clean tea towel. If you cover them as soon as they come out of the pan, the parathas will remain soft and pliable, which is how you want them.

Any uneaten parathas can be reheated by putting them, on top of each other, on a plate, again covered with an upturned bowl (not plastic), and placing them either in an oven preheated to 200°C/180°C fan/gas 6 for about 15 minutes, or by heating them in a hot pan again, covering them immediately afterwards.

STOCKS

Chicken stock

This is probably the most important recipe in the book! I use chicken stock more than any other stock when making soups and broths, as it's got a wonderful flavour but it doesn't overpower or dominate.

The South American proverb 'Bone broth will resurrect the dead', while wildly optimistic, does show how the ancient practice of boiling bones with vegetables in water has been exalted as one of the most nutritious foods for many centuries, worldwide. The better the bones (free-range or organic, which will also be free-range) and vegetables, the better the stock will be. Packed full of goodness, a good bone stock is thought to contain minerals, vitamins, amino acids from the collagen and more, helping our skin, our joints and bones and our digestive system too.

I tend to roast a chicken about once a week at home, so I've always got some chicken stock on the go for soups, sauces and stews. Sometimes my stock is stronger than other times, and will be quite gelatinous when chilled, showing that I've used lots of bones in proportion to water, and other times it'll be lighter.

Once you get into the habit of never wasting the bones and instead just putting them into a pot with a few vegetables, aromatics and lots of water to simmer for a couple of hours, you'll never turn back. No stock cube (however handy they may be from time to time) can compare to a homemade version.

This recipe is just a guideline: you can add so many different herbs and vegetables to the stockpot, depending on the flavour of stock that you love. It's a great way to use up leek or fennel tops, a mushroom or two, or some leftover sprigs of herbs, even a little ginger peel. Try not to add too much of any one vegetable, though, or the flavour may dominate the stock. Livers and any blood are unwelcome, as they will make the stock bitter, but necks, gizzards (the muscle found in the digestive tract of a bird), hearts and wing tips are perfect for stocks. Chicken feet will also greatly enhance a stock or broth.

It's important to use cold water when making a stock, as it will draw the flavour and goodness out of the bones and vegetables while it heats up in the pot. Avoid starchy vegetables such as potatoes, turnips, celeriac or parsnips, as they will simply disintegrate and make the stock cloudy.

If you want to cook a stock for a whole day, you can use a slow cooker, which is perfect for making a stock, or even pop your stock that's been simmering on the hob into the oven at 100°C/80°C fan/gas ½ if you prefer.

This recipe can be used for any bird – wild game or domesticated poultry. If I'm making a duck or goose stock, I love to roast the bare bones, even if the whole bird was roasted beforehand, as the deep, rich flavour is greatly enhanced. You can roast chicken and other bird bones before making a stock too, but I prefer not to. See the duck stock recipe (see page 268).

A really good way to tell when the stock is ready, i.e. when it has cooked enough, is to taste a scrap of meat from the bones, or some of the vegetables. If there's still flavour in the meat or vegetables, then it hasn't given all that it's got to give, just yet, so cook it some more. When you are satisfied that all the flavour from the meat and vegetables is in the liquid itself, it's ready to strain.

I like to add a pinch of salt to my chicken stock to season it from the very beginning, but some people don't. Do whichever you wish.

What is the difference between broth and stock? Some people interchange the two names for the same thing, but technically a traditional bone broth will take 12–24 hours to cook over a very low heat, and it will sometimes have 1 tablespoon of vinegar added to it to extract the maximum goodness from the bones. Having said that, a clear soup that hasn't been blended with other ingredients can also be called a broth, as is the case with many of the recipes in this book.

If you have chicken bones and don't have time (however quick it is to make) to put on a stock, pop the bones into the freezer, whether they're raw or cooked. You can add to them in the freezer whenever you like and then make one big batch of stock at your convenience, using a mixture of cooked and raw bones or just one or the other.

I adore a cup of hot chicken stock with nothing added but a pinch of salt to season, but then, of course, once you've made your stock you have a million different opportunities to explore with different soups, stews and sauces using this golden nectar.

►

GF

1 chicken carcass or whatever chicken bones you have, cooked or raw

1–2 medium carrots, scrubbed clean and halved

1–2 onions, halved, or 4–6 spring onions

1 leek, or even just the green part

1–2 celery stalks

a bunch of parsley stalks

a sprig of thyme

a small bay leaf

a few black peppercorns

a pinch of salt (optional)

Put all the ingredients into a large saucepan and add enough cold water to cover everything by about 8cm. Bring to the boil, then lower the heat and simmer for about 2 or 3 hours, skimming the froth from the top from time to time. Sometimes I don't get to do this, but the 'broth purists' will say that it gives you a clearer stock if you do. To be honest, I don't worry about it – my stock is normally lovely and clear anyway.

Next, strain the stock so you are left with just the liquid, and discard the vegetables and any bones. Allow to cool, then place in the fridge. If you want to use the stock straight away you need to lift the fat off the top and discard it, then it's ready to use. It can be a bit of a fiddle skimming the unchilled fat off the stock, but if you want to use it immediately, it's necessary; normally, though, I place it in the fridge, where the fat will chill and almost harden, which makes it much easier to remove. However, I do not remove the fat until I want to use the stock, as I find that it keeps very well (for a few weeks) in the fridge with the layer of fat sitting on top, as this seals it.

To clarify your stock if it's looking a bit cloudier than you want it to be, pour it through a sieve lined with a piece of kitchen paper, into a bowl or jug underneath.

If you're not sure if your stock is still fresh, boil a little bit of it – if it froths greatly, that can be a sign that it's gone off. To be sure, just taste a little – you'll know immediately if it's gone off. I remember my grandmother showing me that trick.

 notes *If you wish to concentrate the flavour, place the strained and degreased stock in a pan on a high heat and boil, uncovered, to reduce it. If you reduce it to about a quarter of its original volume (it should taste quite strong), you can, once cool, pour it into ice cube trays, then freeze, giving you your own frozen stock cubes.*

Stock can be frozen for up to a year. After that it will begin to lose some flavour but will not pose a health risk.

Asian chicken stock

If I'm making a chicken stock specifically for an Asian broth, I'll follow the previous recipe but will add a few slices of ginger and lots of coriander stalks (and roots, if I can get them) to the stock, leaving the coriander leaves to add to the broth when serving.

I find that duck stock (and goose stock too) really benefits from roasting the carcasses or bones first, whether the whole bird has been previously roasted, or not. It gives it a sweeter, deeper flavour that is rich and delicious.

Roasted duck stock

Makes approximately 3 litres

1 duck carcass, and any leftover bones
3 large, unpeeled cloves of garlic
1 onion, peeled and cut in half
1 small leek, cut in half
1 carrot, scrubbed clean and halved
a bunch of parsley stalks
a sprig of thyme
a pinch of salt

First preheat the oven to 230°C/210°C fan/gas 8. Break apart the duck carcass into 2 or 3 pieces. Put the carcass and any bones on a roasting tray, spread out in a single layer. Place the garlic cloves on a work surface and bash them with a rolling pin or something heavy to break them up slightly. Add to the duck bones on the roasting tray, then place in the hot oven and roast for 10–15 minutes, until the duck bones are deep golden around the edges.

Put the duck bones into a large saucepan. Put the roasting tray over a medium to high heat and add about 400ml of water, using a whisk to dissolve (deglaze) the juices that have stuck to the bottom of the tray. Once it's all dissolved, pour all the liquid into the saucepan with the bones and add the onion, leek, carrot, parsley and thyme. Season with a pinch of salt and top up with cold water to cover the bones by a good few centimetres. Place on a medium heat and bring to the boil. Lower the heat and continue to simmer for 2–3 hours, skimming any froth off the top of the liquid while it simmers away. It's not the end of the world if you don't skim the stock while it's simmering – it might be slightly cloudy from no skimming, but will still be just as delicious.

If the water evaporates in cooking, make sure to top it up in order to keep the vegetables and bones well submerged.

To see if the stock is cooked enough, taste a little scrap of the meat on the bones – if it still has flavour it means it needs longer cooking. When cooked, all the flavour from the meat and bones, and the vegetables too, will have transferred to the liquid. Strain the stock.

Allow to cool, then place in the fridge. If the stock has time to chill in the fridge, the fat that rises to the top while it's cooling will set, making it easy to lift off (and save for roast potatoes another time).

prepare ahead

Duck stock will keep in the fridge for up to 2 weeks, particularly if covered with a layer of fat, and it can be frozen for up to 6 months.

Asian duck stock

If I'm making a duck stock specifically for an Asian broth, I'll follow the previous recipe but will add a few slices of ginger (unpeeled) and lots of coriander stalks (and roots, if I can get them) to the stock, leaving the coriander leaves to add to the broth when serving.

Goose stock

To make a goose stock, do the same as in the duck stock recipe but use double the vegetables and aromatics, as the goose carcass and bones are larger than that of the duck.

Game stock

If I'm making a game stock, I'll follow the recipe above but include whatever game I have – partridge, grouse, pheasant or quail all work well. As with the duck or goose stock, roasting the carcasses or bones first, whether or not the whole bird has been previously roasted, gives a deeper flavour.

Beef (or lamb) stock

A deliciously hearty stock that I also love to drink as a broth from a cup, just as it is, simply seasoned with a pinch of salt. Long, slow cooking is what you're looking for here, and you'll get a wonderful stock from cooking it for 5–6 hours, but if you want to extract practically every bit of flavour and goodness from the bones, then cook the stock for an even longer amount of time. It can also be cooked in a simmering oven (at 120°C/100°C fan/gas ½) or in a slow cooker, for 12–18 hours.

2.5kg beef (or lamb) bones, ideally
   with some scraps of meat on

4 onions, unpeeled, halved

2 large carrots, cut into large chunks

3 celery stalks, cut into large chunks

a large bouquet garni (including a
   few parsley stalks, 1 small bay leaf
   and 3 sprigs of thyme)

10 black peppercorns

6 unpeeled cloves of garlic, cut in half

1 tablespoon tomato purée

Preheat the oven to 230°C/210°C fan/gas 8.

Put the bones in a single layer on a roasting tray, then place in the preheated oven and roast for 30 minutes, or until the bones are well browned. Add the onions, carrots and celery, nestled among the bones, and return the roasting tray to the oven until the vegetables are also browned, another 20–30 minutes.

Take the roasting tray out of the oven and tip the bones and vegetables into a large saucepan. Place the roasting tray on the hob over a medium to high heat. Pour in some water, about 400ml, and deglaze by using a whisk to scrape any roasting juices from the bottom of the tray, allowing them to dissolve into the water as it heats up. Once the water and any remaining juices have come to the boil, pour this over the bones and vegetables in the saucepan.

Add the bouquet garni, peppercorns, garlic and tomato purée. Add about 3½ litres of water and bring slowly to the boil. Skim off any froth that rises to the surface, then lower the heat and simmer gently for 5–6 hours, topping up with water if it reduces too much while boiling. Strain the stock, set aside to cool, then place in the fridge to chill. The fat is easy to lift off the top of the stock once it has chilled. This stock will freeze well.

Fish stock

Fish stock is a quick stock to make, taking under 1 hour in total. Ask your fishmonger for fresh fish bones, and if you don't have time to make the stock straight away, pop the bones into the freezer for another day. The bones with the richest flavour are those of turbot, brill, John Dory and black sole (Dover sole), but failing that, any good fresh white fish bones will be next best. I also like to use some salmon bones in my fish stock, for their depth of flavour.

You can use fish heads if the gills have been removed – just cut the gills away from both sides of the fish head, then pull them out and discard.

If I have some fennel bulb trimmings, I'll add those to my fish stock too, when I add the other vegetables.

15g butter

150g onions, finely sliced

1 celery stalk, sliced

1 leek, trimmed and sliced

1.5kg fish bones, heads and tails, gills removed

250ml dry white wine

4 black peppercorns

1 sprig of thyme

4–5 parsley stalks

½ a small bay leaf

Place a large saucepan over a medium heat and add the butter. Allow to melt, then tip in the sliced onions, celery and leek, toss, and turn the heat down to low. Cover with a butter wrapper or a piece of parchment paper, and the saucepan lid, and cook the vegetables for approximately 10 minutes, until soft but not coloured. You may need to stir a couple of times while they're cooking to prevent them sticking to the base of the pan.

While the vegetables are cooking, cut the bones into large chunks, using a cleaver or a large heavy knife. Wash them thoroughly under cold running water until no trace of blood remains, then add them to the saucepan. Turn the heat up to high and stir the bones while they cook with the onions, celery and leek for a few minutes, until they're turning opaque around the edges. Make sure not to burn the vegetables.

Add the wine and boil, uncovered, until it has just evaporated. Cover with 2 litres of cold water, and add the peppercorns and the herbs. Bring to the boil, then lower the heat and simmer for 30 minutes, skimming often. Strain and allow to cool. Then place in the fridge – once it's chilled you'll be able to skim off any fat easily before using.

Asian-style fish stock

The ginger, garlic and coriander bring such aromatic goodness to this fish stock, which is ideal for using in soups with Eastern/Asian flavours.

Makes approximately 2–2.5 litres

750g fish bones, heads and tails, gills removed

150g onions, sliced

3 spring onions, roughly chopped

1 celery stalk, sliced

50g fresh ginger, unpeeled, sliced

4 large cloves of garlic, peeled and sliced

a large handful of coriander roots and stems, roughly chopped

4 black peppercorns

Wash the fish bones and heads well under cold running water to remove any trace of blood, then place in a large saucepan and add all the remaining ingredients. Pour in 3 litres of cold water, bring to the boil over a medium to high heat, then reduce the heat to a gentle simmer, skimming the surface to remove (and discard) any froth that appears. This will ensure a clear stock. Simmer the stock, uncovered, for 30 minutes, skimming regularly.

Strain the stock and allow to cool. Then place in the fridge and once it's chilled you'll be able to skim off any fat easily before using.

Shellfish stock

To make a shellfish stock, follow the recipe for fish stock but use shellfish shells (or half shellfish and half fish bones), such as those from prawns or shrimps. If you're using large lobster or crayfish, or crabs, you will need to crack the shells well with a hammer or mallet.

note

If a very clear stock is needed, pour it through a sieve lined with kitchen paper before using.

Dashi

Makes approximately 1 litre

The Asian stock known as dashi is an integral component of so many Japanese dishes. It forms the base for miso soup, noodle broths and many sauces. It delivers a characteristic savoury (or umami) flavour, which is a cornerstone of much Japanese cuisine.

 GF

a 10 x 10cm piece of konbu
25g bonito flakes

Wipe the konbu with dry kitchen paper to remove any dust, but don't wash it or the umami flavour will be lost. Put a litre of cold water into a saucepan and add the konbu. Allow it to soak for 30 minutes to 1 hour (opt for the hour if you have time).

Put the pan of water on a high heat and just before it comes to the boil, take out the konbu. The stock you have left is konbu dashi.

Put the water back on the heat and add the bonito flakes, stir, then turn off the heat and allow to sit for 10 minutes.

Pour the broth through a strainer, but don't push the bonito flakes through as it will make the broth too strong.

 note *You can use this stock when it is clear and tasty. It will keep for 2–3 days in the fridge.*

Chinese stock

Makes approximately 5 litres

This delicious, light but full-flavoured stock is excellent in Chinese fish or meat soups. If you want to make it pork-free, use a total of 2kg of chicken carcasses, wings and giblets.

1.25kg chicken carcasses, wings and giblets (necks, hearts, gizzards, etc.)

750g pork spare ribs

40g piece of fresh ginger, unpeeled, sliced into 10 pieces

6 large spring onions

50ml Shaoxing rice wine

Put the chicken and pork pieces into a large saucepan with the ginger, spring onions and 5 litres of cold water and place over a medium to high heat. Bring to the boil, skimming off any froth that appears on the surface as it heats up. This is to ensure a clear glossy stock.

Now, lower the heat and simmer gently for about 3–4 hours, skimming every hour or so, until the flavour from the scraps of meat has been transferred into the liquid. Top up with more cold water if the water evaporates – the bones should be covered with water at all times.

Add the rice wine and allow to cool. Strain the stock, then refrigerate. Once it's cold the fat will solidify, making it much easier to lift it off the top.

Remove the solidified fat from the top of the stock before use. The stock will keep in the fridge for at least a week, and it also freezes perfectly.

 note *Simmer the stock uncovered if a really clear stock is needed. I also like to pour it through a sieve lined with kitchen paper just before using it if I find that it's not quite clear enough.*

Stocks – soup broth bread   275

Vegetable stock

This recipe is really just a rough guide, depending on what ingredients you have. Don't think of this, though, as a means of recycling any old vegetable from the fridge. Potatoes don't have much to offer a stock and they just make it cloudy. Turnips and parsnips can be too strong in flavour, as can cauliflower, broccoli and Brussels sprouts.

I often add garlic cloves, still in their skins, just cut in half, to a vegetable stock, and sometimes even fresh coriander sprigs and a couple of slices of ginger – it depends on what recipe I am using the stock for, whether I'll introduce Asian flavours or not.

2 onions, peeled and roughly sliced

2 whole leeks, the base trimmed, or the green tops of 3–4 leeks

4 celery stalks, cut into large chunks

3 large carrots, scrubbed and cut into chunks

½ a fennel bulb, cut into chunks

a handful of mushrooms, quartered, or mushroom stalks

4–6 parsley stalks

2 large sprigs of thyme

1 small bay leaf

a few peppercorns

Place all the vegetables in a large saucepan and add the herbs and peppercorns. Pour in 3 litres of cold water, making sure there is enough to cover the vegetables well. Place on a high heat, bring to the boil, then lower the heat, cover the pan with a lid and allow to simmer for 1–1½ hours, until flavoursome. Strain through a sieve.

This stock keeps for 2 weeks in the fridge and can be frozen.

Ramen broth

Makes approximately 4 litres

Making your own ramen broth is a labour of love. It takes a long, long time for the broth to cook, but you can get on with other things while it's bubbling away. This broth recipe makes a lot, about 4 litres, which will feed about 10 people, but you can freeze whatever you don't use, and it's just as easy to make lots as it is to make a small amount, provided you have a large enough saucepan. Once the broth is made, the rest of the ramen is straightforward and fairly quick to put together, not to mention completely and utterly delicious.

There are countless regional variations of ramen, typically categorized by their soup base, although variations that combine different bases are not uncommon. Some cooks leave out the first stage of boiling and discarding the water from the bones; however, I do include that stage, else I find there's a lot to skim from the top of the broth when it's cooking. Traditionally, dashi is added to the broth as well, and while this is what the purists will do, admittedly sometimes I don't.

This recipe is based on a tonkotsu ramen broth, which is made with pork bones: pork hock or trotters, or both, and often with seafood stock added too (though I have not added it in this recipe). The pork bones are boiled for many hours (at least 8, and sometimes even for a few days), until the collagen and fat break down and liquefy. The collagen that's found in the bones, and in the tendons that surround the bones, makes the broth incredibly nutritious and flavoursome with an opaque appearance. When cold, this broth will be like a stiffly set jelly, but it will be beautifully silken when hot.

I make a tonkotsu-style broth using pigs' trotters (very inexpensive from your butcher) and chicken carcasses. I also include some pork shoulder, which brings flavour to the broth and also cooks in it and can then be shredded and crisped up in a frying pan – a delicious topping for the ramen. If you are using ramen broth from your freezer, I recommend slow-roasting a chunk of shoulder or belly of pork until it's meltingly tender, so that you can shred it and crisp it up in a pan, as in the sticky pork with sesame recipe (see page 205).

If the thought of making a broth that needs a whole day to cook is just too much for you, you could use a really good chicken stock instead for an unauthentic version. But it'll still be a delicious bowl of goodness. While not traditional, I do sometimes place the covered saucepan in the oven, preheated to 100°C/80°C fan/gas ½, to cook the broth if I want to get the pan out of the way.

GF

2kg pigs' trotters, split in half lengthwise (ask your butcher to do this)

1kg chicken carcasses

2 tablespoons olive oil (vegetable oil is traditionally used, but I use olive oil)

2 large onions, peeled and cut into quarters

2 large leeks, cut into large chunks

1 head of garlic, unpeeled cloves separated and bashed with the base of a small saucepan to just open/split them

50g piece of fresh ginger, unpeeled, cut into 5mm slices

750g piece of skinless and boneless pork shoulder (not cut up)

First, place the pigs' trotters and chicken carcasses in a large saucepan and cover well with cold water. Bring to the boil and boil over a high heat for 2 minutes, then strain the bones, discarding the liquid. Wash the bones under cold running water to remove all traces of blood and any dark matter. This is the key to making a milky broth.

Next, place the large saucepan over a high heat again. Add the olive or vegetable oil and allow to get hot, then toss in the onion quarters, leek chunks, the bashed garlic cloves and the sliced ginger and stir over a high heat until browned around the edges. Now put back the pigs' trotters and the chicken carcasses, along with the pork shoulder (still in one piece). Pour in plenty of cold water to cover, about 6 litres. Cover with a lid and bring to the boil. In the first 20 minutes of boiling, remove the lid a few times and skim off and discard any scum/froth that comes to the surface, then continue to cook, still covered, at a slow rolling boil (rather than lightly simmering, increasing or decreasing the heat slightly to adjust the boiling speed), for approximately 3 hours, until the pork shoulder is very tender and almost falling apart. Remove the pork shoulder, setting it aside in the fridge for making your ramen (see page 117).

Continue to cook the broth, still covered and at a slow rolling boil, until the broth is opaque, about 6–7 hours altogether, or longer if you wish, topping up as necessary with water to keep the bones well submerged at all times.

When the broth is cooked, turn off the heat, let it cool slightly, then remove the bones and strain the liquid through a colander into a large bowl. Now line a large sieve with a thin sheet of kitchen paper (or use a jelly bag) and pour the strained broth through it – this way you'll get a wonderfully bit-free broth.

Allow the broth to cool, then skim all the fat from the top. This is made really easy if you make the broth a day or more in advance (it'll keep in the fridge for a week or more), then spoon off the set chilled fat and discard. The broth will have set to a firm jelly. If you're chilling the broth, cover the pork shoulder and chill this also.

Index

Thanks

I adore the process of writing a cookbook. From the stage where ideas are thrown out on the table to seeing the book come to full fruition, with all the recipe-testing, writing, designing, shooting and editing in between – I love it all.

I have been so lucky to have worked with many of the people involved in this project before, and to have met new super talents too.

My great friend (and ex-publisher) Jenny Heller is now my wonderful agent at Robertson Murray, the literary arm of Arlington Enterprises. Thank you all for getting as excited as I am about this new book and for joining me on this next stage.

Ione Walder, it is just brilliant to work with you again. Thanks so much to you and your fabulous team at Penguin Michael Joseph; you have expertly and kindly cajoled me to get this book finished (almost) on time. Claire Collins, Emma Henderson, Annie Lee, you are all saints, and very patient and professional ones too, so thank you. A massive thanks also to Gaby Young, Sophie Shaw, Gail Jones, Daniel Prescott-Bennett and Beth O'Rafferty.

I had a very clear picture in my mind from the start of how I wanted the cover and overall design of this book to look, so I'm eternally grateful to Sarah Fraser for understanding my vision and making it work, and for Jessica Hart's beautiful illustrations. I'm so grateful to have had Maya Smend, Annie Rigg, Lydia McPherson, Jo Murphy, Cliodhna Prendergast and Liz McCarthy all on board to create such beautiful images; you are all fabulous geniuses. A big cosy cashmere kiss to Lucy Downes of Sphere One for letting me wear her divine cashmeres for this shoot and every day.

A big shout out to Carrie Anderson, Cliona Lewis, Louise Farrell and Laura Dermody who keep the Penguin show on the road here in Ireland, thank you.

I feel so much gratitude to my loving and inspiring parents-in-law, Tim and Darina, Rory O'Connell and all of our fabulous crew at Ballymaloe, without whom I would not be teaching cooking and doing what I love.

 And to my cherished direct and extended family, and my fabulous friends who support me with so much love and help to enrich my life, thank you darlings.